Monk's Musings
FAITH, LIFE, NOTRE DAME

Mike,

In appreciation of
your friendship and
colleagueship in Holy Cross.

Monk

Monk's Musings
FAITH, LIFE, NOTRE DAME

BY
EDWARD A. MALLOY, C.S.C.

Foreword by
Rev. John I. Jenkins, C.S.C.

Monk's Musings

ISBN 978-1-7321150-1-9

Cover photos: Matt Cashore

Published by
Corby Books
A Division of Corby Publishing LP
P.O. Box 93
Notre Dame, Indiana 46556

Manufactured in the United States of America

TABLE OF CONTENTS

Theological Reflections

PART TWO
LIFE

Reflections on Virtues in the Christian Life

Reflections on War and Peace

PART THREE
NOTRE DAME

Reflections on Notre Dame

Occasional Musings

FOREWORD

Fr. Malloy was my predecessor as President of Notre Dame, and Fr. Hesburgh was Fr. Malloy's predecessor. Since becoming president of Notre Dame, I have often sought Fr. Malloy's advice, as I did Fr. Hesburgh's before his passing. Both men have been unfailingly generous in offering me their fraternal support and counsel both practical and wise. For that I am and always will be deeply grateful.

Most of us know Fr. Malloy as "Monk." Among Monk's many admirable qualities is one trait that stands out to me—his extraordinary powers of observation. Monk notices and reflects on the things we often miss. He sees the significance of those small but important details that often do not even enter the minds of the rest of us. This skill for noticing contributes to his ability to size up people and events.

When I go to Monk to discuss a matter or seek his counsel, he has a wealth of observations, small and large, relevant to the matter at hand. He has a remarkable ability to recall the particulars of a given situation or important details about a person. While he makes it look effortless, this capacity to notice each person and the world around him is a rare gift, one that requires great patience and discipline. It requires a real attentiveness to the world around.

In the pages that follow, the reader has the opportunity to benefit from Monk's gift for noticing and reflecting on what is seen. This book will allow the reader to benefit from those gifts as I have.

Rev. John I. Jenkins, C.S.C.
PRESIDENT, UNIVERSITY OF NOTRE DAME

PREFACE

After finishing my three-volume memoir, *Monk's Tale*, I was intent on writing a shorter book with shorter chapters. So, I began reflecting about a wide variety of topics. I drew upon classes I had taught, talks I had given, retreats that I had preached, and other material that was of interest to me. With the assistance of Jim Langford, I began to put together sections of material that constituted a related whole. This book is the result of those efforts.

It is free of the usual scholarly apparatus. However, I want to acknowledge and thank the many authors who have informed and influenced my own thinking.

The word "musing" in the title is intended to suggest a kind of brevity of treatment of the subject of each chapter. I have, in fact, pondered, thought about, and engaged these issues much more extensively in my life as a teacher, scholar and pastor. My hope is that busy people and non-academics might enjoy and benefit from a more circumscribed version of my own reflections.

PART ONE

FAITH

BIBLICAL REFLECTIONS

In this section, I offer rather brief reflections on central material from the Hebrew (Old Testament) and Christian (New Testament) Scriptures. It is my intention to make scholarly work available in a simple format that might touch wider human experience.

Mark the Evangelist

By scholarly consensus, the Gospel of Mark is the first among the four Christian Gospels. It is the briefest in its modern version at sixteen short chapters. It seems to have been addressed to pagan converts.

One of the interesting questions of Biblical history is why we have no writings of Jesus himself. It would seem that it would have been more effective for Jesus to, in a sense, certify the memory he left behind. But, as we well know from the way he gathered his disciples together and empowered them at Pentecost, it was they who were to be agents of the word and exemplars of the Gospel in subsequent generations. There was, of course, a long process by which the four extant Gospels were embraced by the Church universal. There were other Gospels circulating in the early centuries of the Church, but none of them won the same level of acceptance.

Mark's Gospel is not only characterized by its briefness but also by several other aspects. Unlike Matthew and Luke, it has no infancy narrative. It begins with the ministry of John the Baptist and the pivotal moment of Jesus' baptism by John in the Jordan

River. There are several themes that wind themselves through the text. One was that his audiences were living at the end of history as we know it. All things were to be made new. Not surprisingly, it was frequently the case that the disciples misunderstood what Jesus was teaching them. Only after his resurrection and the coming of the Holy Spirit at Pentecost would his followers begin to comprehend the power and beauty of his message.

I would like to focus on two themes in Mark's Gospel: (1) Miracles and (2) Jesus as the suffering servant.

Miracles

A miracle can be understood as an extraordinary event manifesting divine intervention in human affairs. In the context of Mark's Gospel, a miracle is the manifestation of the power of the Kingdom of God. It is intended to either invoke faith or reinforce existing faith. We see a multiplicity of miracles by Jesus in the Gospel. Some are intended for individual people (not to speak of the onlookers) and others for groups of people. Those who are healed are seen to be suffering from possession by the devil and various illnesses (including leprosy, paralysis, a withered hand, a hemorrhage, deafness, blindness, and epilepsy). We also see Jesus calming the waters of the Sea of Galilee in a storm, multiplying the loaves and fishes in order to feed the crowd, walking on water and again multiplying the loaves in order to feed the crowd.

We know from Jesus' temptations in the desert that he never intended to present himself primarily as a miracle worker. In a sense, these were adjuncts to his message. There were people who saw the miracles but did not become believers. At a minimum, the acceptance of miracles requires openness to wonder and awe and personal humility. If we have eyes to see, we can recognize that there are, in one sense or another, miracles in everyday life, like the birth of a baby, the beauty of nature, the experiences of conversion and forgiveness, human creativity, various forms of heroism, including martyrdom, and even the survival of the Church for two millennia.

In contemporary life, you don't want to be too easily taken in by false claims of miraculous power from those who would take advantage of us. We still have the need for evidence and rational analysis. But, not unlike people in every generation, we need to be open at the same time to the wonders of God's presence in our lives and in our world.

Jesus as the Suffering Servant

In Mark's Gospel we see Jesus make three predictions of his passion. Included in his message on these occasions are themes that will resonate throughout the Gospel. We need to lose our life to save it. The greatest need is to be the servants of the rest. The only way to eternal glory is the way of the cross. Jesus' crucifixion and death are not the end of the story; rather, the resurrection is.

There is obviously a sense of irony and paradox built into the Christian mystery. That we begin our formal prayer with the sign of the cross, that we have crucifixes on our walls and in the fronts of churches, and that we celebrate the various stages of Jesus' journey to the cross during Holy Week are all rather strange in the eyes of outsiders. To see Jesus as our Suffering Servant and to recognize the great reversal at the end of time when the last shall be first and the first last, these are utterly counter-cultural in their significance.

As I've grown older, I am of the conviction that none of us has to look very far to find our own personal crosses. This can involve our sickness or that of those we love. It can be in the aftermath of the death of a loved one. It can be the result of disappointment in human relationships. For some among us this can include unemployment or underemployment, homelessness, various forms of addiction, the loss of reputation, chronic depression or mental illness, the onset of dementia, being victims of various natural disasters, being afflicted by war or famine, and a very contemporary one, being affected by various forms of criminality and/or terrorism.

The question is not whether we will know suffering, pain, and the reality of the cross in our personal lives, but rather how we deal with it. If we follow Jesus' example we can recognize the connection between the cross and the path to eternal glory. We are called to be people of hopefulness no matter what kinds of difficulty we face. And for all the good fortune we might enjoy, we have a correlative responsibility to assist others in their need.

As a member of the Congregation of Holy Cross our motto is in Latin, "*ave crux, spes unica*" or "*behold the cross, our only hope.*" I think this little motto is very consistent with one of the messages at the heart of Mark's Gospel.

The Gospel of Matthew

Historically, the Gospel of Matthew was attributed to Matthew the tax collector. It is surely intended for a Jewish audience and is dependent on Mark's Gospel and various circulating oral texts. It follows the general pattern of Mark's Gospel with the major differences being the nativity narratives and the resurrection and commissioning accounts. There is a heavy stress on the mission of the Church to the Jews.

There are several themes worth noting:

- ❀ *Jesus is seen as the fulfillment* of the law and the prophets, that is, Yahweh's promise to the chosen people. Matthew sites the Old Testament 41 times, which clearly indicates that the author expected the readers to be familiar with these texts.

- ❀ *Jesus is seen as the teacher* of a higher kind of righteousness. His two main adversaries are the teachers of Judaism, who seem threatened by his approach to the law, and Christians who reject the law entirely. That is why we hear that Jesus came to fulfill the law and the prophets.

There are five great discourses in Matthew's Gospel. Jesus is seen as a teacher, much like Moses was to the people of Israel in the Hebrew Scriptures. These oral deliveries include: the Sermon on the Mount, the Missionary Discourse, the teaching about Parables, various community regulations, and words about the End of Time. As a result of these discourses, Matthew quotes the words of Jesus more frequently than do the other Gospels.

❀ *The structure of the Gospel*—One of the distinctive features of Matthew's Gospel is the Infancy Narrative. Mark lacks this material and biblical commentators have speculated that there was a great interest in the early Church about Jesus' origins. As a result, both Matthew and Luke have presentations about Jesus' roots. In Matthew we have the genealogy followed by the description of the birth and the visit of the Magi, the flight into Egypt and the killing of the Holy Innocents. These are all seen as the fulfillment of various scriptural prophecies. The second element of great significance is the Sermon on the Mount, which I will deal with separately. It is surely the best known of all of the major sections of Matthew's Gospel. Another feature of the Gospel is the frequency of Jesus' teaching in parables. Matthew has Jesus explain why this distinctive form of storytelling was designed as an appropriate way to convey spiritual truth. Another dimension is the continual clash between Jesus and the Jewish religious authorities. This included discussions about paying taxes to the Romans, the nature of the Resurrection, and the Great Commandment of love of God and neighbor. The harshest language in the Gospels spoken by Jesus is directed toward the Pharisees who bound the people to the strictest interpretation of the law but missed the fundamental spiritual values that underlay it. Matthew also pictures the destruction of Jerusalem as a judgment from God. The final dimension of Matthew's Gospel worth discussing is his Apostolic Commission to the disciples. They were to preach the Good News to all the world. After the Resurrection, they have the power and authority of the Risen Lord.

In summary, we can say that Matthew's Gospel is full of Jesus' profound teaching and proclaims that he is the one who was promised as the Messiah to bring the fulfillment both of law and the prophets. That is why the name Jesus Christ, which suggests etymologically that he is both Redeemer and The Promised One, is a revelatory name indeed.

The Sermon on the Mount

When it comes to the four Gospels, there is no extended text that has received more attention, not only from Christian commentators, but also outside of the Christian community, than what has been called the Sermon on the Mount (Matthew 5:1-7:27). Luke's Gospel has a comparable text, sometimes called the Discourse on the Plain, which resembles the Sermon on the Mount but seems, in the end, less profound.

The Sermon on the Mount draws continual parallels between Moses on Mount Sinai receiving the Old Law from Yahweh and Jesus on the Mount of the Beatitudes proclaiming the New Law to his disciples. This similarity would have been inherently obvious to a Jewish audience. Most commentators suggest that the Sermon is a device to gather together a number of Jesus' sayings which were given in a variety of settings. As a result, we can see it as historical in general but not having taken place all on one occasion.

The components of the Sermon include:

❋ *The Beatitudes*—This section is the keynote of the Sermon in which Jesus offers eight beatitudes or blessings for those who strive to live a holy life. Each of the values proclaimed in the Beatitudes is opposed to the conventional ones that prevailed in both the Jewish and Roman worlds. Among the blessed are the poor in spirit, those who mourn, the merciful, the peacemakers, those who are gentle, those who hunger and thirst for what is right, the pure in heart, and those persecuted in the cause of right. Mahatma Gandhi once said that the Beatitudes would be an extraordinary way to live one's life and he admired this aspect of Christian teaching but seldom saw it put into practice by the Christians he encountered.

❋ *The Community is called to be "The Salt of the Earth" and "The Light of the World"*—These beautiful images suggest that the followers of Jesus have a significant role to play in the world, both by their example and by their active involvement.

❧ *The Six Antitheses of the Law*—Jesus suggests that he came not to abolish the law but to complete it and the antitheses push us to understand the inner temptations that can lead us astray. For example, uncontrolled anger can lead to the killing of another human, our lust can lead to the practice of adultery, our commitment in marital relations should be firm, we should not rely on oaths to prove our veracity, we should leave behind our temptation to retaliation and learn to turn the other cheek, and we should not just love our friends, but also strive to love our enemies. Each of these antitheses are ways of thinking about the Christian call to perfection. Even when we fail to realize this high ethic, we can see it as an aspiration and a common goal.

❧ *Reflection on various acts of piety*—The three great pillars of Jewish piety were almsgiving, prayer, and fasting. Jesus encourages these, but also warns about the danger of apostasy and excessive ostentation. It is important in this light not to seek recognition for our inner spiritual practices but rather to engage in them with a proper disposition. The Lord's Prayer or the Our Father is given by Jesus as a model kind of prayer in which we first acknowledge the priority of God in our lives and then seek God's support for our basic needs.

❧ *The Sermon on the Mount* concludes with a number of isolated sayings that include: we cannot serve both God and money; we should not judge and therefore will not be judged (ourselves;) in prayer we should ask, seek and knock; and the encouragement to practice the "Golden Rule," that is, treat others as we would have them treat ourselves.

❧ *The meaning of the Sermon on the Mount*—The sermon pictures morality as rooted in the inner person, bases it on the universality of love and indicates that the demand is urgent that we live by a new morality. All of it only makes sense in light of faith and a life of discipleship. It has more to do with an orientation of our life than it does with specific rules.

Some have seen the Sermon as an ethic of perfection to be taken literally and applied absolutely and universally. The vast majority of Christians, however, have seen it as an ethic of aspiration to be pursued as an ideal and hopefully realized little by little. And others have focused on the Sermon as an ethic of repentance. It is a reminder of our human sinfulness and limitation and that only God can save.

The Sermon on the Mount is one of the great moral discourses in human history. It is surely worthy of our continued reflection.

Luke—Acts

There is a general agreement among scripture scholars that Luke, companion and fellow worker of Paul the Apostle, was the author of both the Gospel of Luke and the Acts of the Apostles. They were written sometime between 80-90 AD. The text set a standard of literary excellence. It invoked a larger vocabulary and Luke used, adapted, and rearranged material freely. In the big picture of things, the story of the Gospel begins in Galilee and ends in Jerusalem and then in Acts, it goes from Jerusalem to Rome. There is a strong sense that the end of the world has been delayed indefinitely and that the Church must live in the world and witness to it. After the Destruction of Jerusalem and the Temple, the Church inevitably spread out to other lands.

There are certain themes that are common to Luke—Acts, which include:

- *The proper use of wealth*—Christians are seen to have a necessity to give generously to the poor. There is also a stress on friendship and hospitality where there will be no division on social economic grounds among the Christian disciples.
  Jesus' followers are called to a way of total renunciation of worldly goods.

- *Mercy for sinners*—There are numerous examples in Luke's Gospel of Jesus' mission of mercy directed toward sinners. In Chapter Seven, Jesus' feet are anointed by a sinful woman and he offers her forgiveness for her sins. In Chapter Fifteen, we have the inter-related parables of the Lost Sheep, the Lost Coin, and the Lost Son (or the Prodigal Son). We also have the story of Zacchaeus, the tax collector, who promised to reform his life and was forgiven by Jesus. The same is true of Jesus granting forgiveness to those who executed him, as well as the good thief, as he was hanging on the cross.

❀ *Prayer*—Throughout Luke's Gospel, Jesus prays before every major step in his ministry. This includes: at the time of his baptism, before the Choice of the Twelve, at the time of the Transfiguration, and in the Garden of Gethsemane. Jesus insists throughout the Gospel that his disciples be people of prayer.

The Holy Spirit—Jesus constantly alludes to the role of the Holy Spirit throughout the Gospel. He will not leave them orphans after he finishes his mission on this earth. At Pentecost, the Spirit empowers the Church to carry on Jesus' mission and history. Thus, we carry on the story of the Gospel into the Acts of the Apostles with a heavy focus on the ministry of Paul the Apostle.

❀ *Women*—More women appear in Luke's Gospel than in the other Gospels. There is also a heavy emphasis on Mary's role in the infancy narratives. This also includes the powerful visitation scene with Elizabeth and Mary before the birth of their children.

Acts of the Apostles

The Acts of the Apostles is the most detailed account of how the Church spread from the land of Israel throughout the Mediterranean region. We see Jerusalem as the sacred city and the home of the traditionalist Christians. Antioch, the third largest city in the Roman Empire, became Paul's mission base. It is said to be the first place where the title "Christians" was applied to the followers of Jesus. Rome, the capital of the empire, was the site of the eventual martyrdoms of Peter and Paul. This, of course, is the root of the center of Christianity moving to Rome eventually. Later on, Ephesus became Paul's main mission station on his travels. And then there is Athens, the Greek cultural center, where Paul appealed to the intellectuals.

Much of the Acts of the Apostles is made up of twenty-eight speeches, which function as a literary device. Many of these talks reflect early Christian mission preaching.

At times, Acts depicts the early Christian community in idyllic terms, especially in contrast to some of Paul's writings, like First Corinthians. It also shows the growth of the Church, little by little, across the regions of the Mediterranean toward the center of the Roman Empire. Another literary device is multiple trial scenes. There are six of them that include the Apostles in general and also Stephen and Paul.

We become familiar with a number of the major figures in Acts. These include: Barnabas, who was the leader of the Church in Antioch and who Paul accompanied early in his mission activity; Cornelius, a Centurion and the first gentile convert; James, a conservative leader of the Church in Jerusalem; Timothy and Silas, who were Paul's regular traveling companions; Ananias and Sapphira, a wealthy couple who had been converted but withheld their goods. They were an example of how not to be a disciple. There was Simon Magus who functioned as a magician and wanted to purchase Paul's sacred powers. That's why we call the attempt to buy Church power for secular purposes the sin of "simony." On the positive side, there was Stephen, the first Christian martyr, who was a deacon; and, of course, the examples of Peter and Paul.

One of the main events in the Acts of the Apostles is the First Council of the Church, the Council of Jerusalem. This led to an agreement between the conservative forces in Jerusalem and Paul and his mission companions that gentile converts would not have to become Jews first. There were some expectations that were passed on but, generally, gentile Christian converts could live consistent with their own backgrounds.

While it is sometimes difficult to follow all of the separate travels of Paul and his companions, the Acts of the Apostles provides a very interesting and lively depiction of the early stages of the growth of the Christian community. In the first twelve chapters, Peter is the hero and, later on, it is Paul. The main theme one can take away from the Acts is how the power of the Spirit was manifest in multiple ways in the mission activity of the apostles and disciples and how fruitful this was in the relatively rapid growth of the Church.

Gospel of John

By consensus, John's Gospel was the last written. It has a much more developed Trinitarian theology. In the Gospel of John, Jesus does not teach through parables and has a three-year (rather than a one-year) ministry before he begins his final journey to Jerusalem. Among the distinctive sections of John's Gospel that do not appear in the other Gospels are the Wedding Feast at Cana, Nicodemus, the Samaritan woman at the well, and the raising of Lazarus.

Much of John's Gospel is like taking a college course in theology. It has long, extended discourses. Like the infancy narratives in Matthew and Luke, the prologue of John's Gospel provides a summary of what is to come in the later chapters.

I would like to focus on three themes in John's Gospel: (1) the seven signs; (2) the "I am" sayings; and (3) the Risen Lord.

The Seven Signs

Unlike Mark's Gospel, for example, John's Gospel has a limited number of accounts of miracles. The so-called Seven Signs include: changing water into wine at Cana, the cure of the official's son at Cana, the cure of the paralytic, the miraculous feeding, Jesus walking on water, the curing of a blind man, and the raising of Lazarus from the dead. All of these are intended to lead up to the ultimate miracle which is, of course, the raising of Jesus from the dead. Each of the signs is intended as evidence in faith that something extraordinary is happening in the presence of Jesus in his public ministry. Jesus provides for his audience a certain insight or an apprehension of the inner nature of things. Some would call these "eureka" or "ah ha" moments. They are all connected to the life of faith in one sense or another. The last of the seven signs, the raising of Lazarus from the dead, is an immediate foreshadowing of Jesus' own resurrection. For example, in Chapter Nine of John's Gospel, which takes up the curing of the blind man, we see Jesus proclaiming himself as the Light of the World. The blind man is cured after Jesus asks him, "Do you have faith in the Son of Man?" He answers, "Lord. I believe." Jesus goes on to say, "I came to give sight to the sightless and to make blind those who see." His opponents are pictured as those who can physically see but are blind religiously. Our call is to see both physically and religiously.

"I am" Sayings

In the "I am" sayings, Jesus identifies himself with the great religious symbols of Israel. He proclaims himself to be: the bread of life; the life; the gate; the good shepherd; the resurrection and the life; the way, truth and life; and the vine.

Take, for example, the image that he is "The way, the truth, and the life." He proclaims that no one comes to the father except by me. We can see the way as a kind of path, route, or direction. It is like having a religious GPS that points out the proper endpoint of our journey. In the early Church, Christians were said to be "participants in the Christian Way of life." Later they were said to be "people on the Way." This image helps us to see life as a journey from the beginning of our existence to death. There are various way stations, perhaps misdirections and detours, but our endpoint is certain.

The truth makes reference to Jesus as the *logos* or Word of God. This is based in the reality or very nature of God. Jesus is opposed to all falsehood, deceit and error. We can literally proclaim, in the university setting, that all paths to truths are ways to the discovery of God. This helps us to understand theology as faith seeking understanding.

Jesus is also the Life; he is the foundation of our ultimate promise and hope. He is opposed to all that would harm, injure, or destroy. Jesus, who is the life, points us beyond death to eternal life.

The Risen Lord

Jesus is also the Risen Lord. At the heart of all of the Gospels is the Passion Narrative with the resurrection accounts. In John's Gospel we move from the empty tomb to multiple appearances, to the commissioning, to Pentecost, to the giving of the power of the Holy Spirit.

Jesus is pictured as making an appearance to Mary Magdalene when Jesus says "Mary:" and she replies "Rabbi." He also appears to the disciples in the upper room where he says, "Peace be with you," "I send you," "Receive the Holy Spirit." He appears to Thomas where he shows him the wounds in his body and Thomas responds, "My Lord and my God." Another appearance is at the Sea of Tiberius where, after a big catch of fish, Jesus serves breakfast to his disciples. Finally, he appears to Simon Peter and asks him, "Do you love me more than these?" After each question, he instructs him to feed his lambs or feed his sheep. In a sense, this is Peter's second chance after his three-fold denial of Jesus prior to his crucifixion. When discussing the resurrection of the Lord we ultimately speak in analogies. We talk about rebirth, the blossoming of nature, the creative spark, blazing insight, and love fulfilled. We look forward to the eternal banquet where we can live forever in the presence of the Living God. This is our ultimate Christian promise and the hope that we have to offer the world.

Paul as an Apostle of the Lord

Saul, educated by the rabbis of his day, is pictured in the Gospels as one who, in his fervor, persecuted the Christian community and was present at the martyrdom of St. Stephen, the first Christian martyr. That is why the picture of his conversion is so dramatic. He had an experience of the resurrected Lord and was blinded after being knocked off his animal. He then went to Antioch where he was trained in the Christian faith. Subsequently, he made three mission journeys preaching first to the Jews and then to the Gentiles. It is clear that his letters were written for specific occasions and audiences. We can guess that he would be utterly surprised to find that his letters have become such an integral part of the Christian scriptures.

Paul did not know Jesus during his public ministry. And yet, he became one of the more profound interpreters of who Jesus was as the Christ. Chronologically, Paul was the first voice and he has had a profound influence on subsequent Christian faith and practice. I would like to stress two themes in Paul's writings: (1) the trials of the Apostolate and (2) the centrality of the Eucharist.

Trials of the Apostolate

We hear in Second Corinthians that all of us who are called to proclaim the Gospel are only earthen vessels. It is not of our own volition that we speak out and try to make Christ known to others. In the process of doing that we should not burden anyone financially. Paul describes in some detail the hardships of his work on behalf of the Gospel. He was imprisoned many times. He was whipped five times with thirty-nine lashes from the Jews, and three times beaten with sticks. He was stoned once and shipwrecked three times. He was once adrift in the open sea for a day and a long night. He was constantly in danger from robbers and brigands and labored frequently without sleep. He knew firsthand what it was to suffer hunger, thirst, and starvation. He knew what it was like to try to travel in the cold without proper clothing. One time he escaped in a basket down the city wall. Even more importantly, he describes a certain "thorn in the flesh," which he three times prayed to be free of. In consolation, he describes a vision he had of paradise.

All of those who take up the work of the Gospel will know trials of one kind or another. We can have incompatible coworkers or lack backing from proper authority. We can have to deal with scandals of one kind or another or feel overworked or lonely. Sometimes our ministry can be affected by ill health of either ourselves or those close to us. We may occasionally feel torn between different points of view within the Church. And then, there are matters related to finances of Churches and other kinds of institutions. And, in our own day in history, we can be depressed by declining Church practice.

All of this is to say that just as Paul had to deal with trials, so all of us will in turn. Some are simply a function of being human but others can be a result of the context in history within which we live and operate. Following the example of Paul we can learn to take up our cross and follow the Lord.

The Centrality of the Eucharist

In First Corinthians, Chapter 11, Paul passes on to us what he had received from the Lord and describes what took place on Holy Thursday at the Last Supper. This feast was foreshadowed by the gift of Manna in the desert in the time of Moses and by the feeding of the multitudes by Jesus along the Sea of Galilee. Christians see the celebration of the Eucharist as a replication of Jesus' table fellowship. It is indeed the prime sacrament of the Church.

The basic structure of the liturgy is highly flexible. There are certain necessary elements like introductory prayers, the penitential rite, readings from Scripture, a homily, preparatory rites, the Consecration, and then the reception of the Eucharist and the concluding prayers. But each of these component parts can be elaborated on by music and various other symbolic rituals. I personally have celebrated Masses or attended those that were twenty minutes long and others that were over two hours. Most marriages take place in the context of the Eucharist and it is a necessary component of the Sacrament of Ordination. The Eucharist can be adapted to the needs of children or the sick or situations of military service or in the context of those who are dying. It can also be celebrated in various language groups utilizing rituals that reflect the local culture. Music is usually a part of the weekly liturgies and sometimes the daily liturgies as well. The music can be of various types even within a given culture.

Some of my greatest memories as a priest are celebrating baptismal Masses, wedding Masses, funeral Masses, and memorial Masses. At Notre Dame, we celebrate almost all of the great occasions with the liturgy like First-Year Orientation, Junior Parents Weekend, and Commencement Weekend. We also have Masses for Alumni Reunion and for special events. One of my most memorable liturgies was on 9/11/01 on the South Quad when we prayed for the victims of the attacks in New York, Virginia, and Pennsylvania and tried to comfort all of the members of our community who experienced so much anxiety on that day. I am happy to say that celebrating the Eucharist and preaching within it is at the heart of my priesthood. I feel very privileged indeed to have been gifted with this opportunity for service in the life of the Church community.

Scriptural Images of Love

There is no theme more characteristic of the teaching and example of Jesus than the instruction to be people of love. Love is not a sentiment, but rather a lived reality. It is one of the most appealing components of the Christian Gospel as preached throughout the ages.

* *The Love Commandment*—In multiple places in the New Testament we hear the refrain, "Love the Lord your God with all of your heart, soul, mind, and strength and your neighbor as yourself." In one way or another this appears in the Gospels of Matthew, Mark, and Luke as well as Paul's Letter to the Romans and Galatians and the Epistle of James. In some ways,

Jesus brought together two separate Jewish teachings into one Commandment. This is not to say that the Jewish Scriptures did not recognize the connection, but rather that Jesus was much more explicit about the relationship between the two components. Jesus taught that the Commandment to love summarizes all of the law and the prophets. In Luke, the so-called Good Samaritan parable immediately follows and makes explicit what love demands, that is, that deeds of love are demanded. Jesus expresses in multiple ways that love is more important than religious performance or cultic activity.

❀ *Love of Enemies*—In both Matthew and Luke we find the instruction "Love your enemies and pray for those who persecute you, bless those who curse you, and pray for those who treat you badly." This difficult and challenging command is intended to imitate the perfection of God. Love demands more than merely tolerating our enemies.

❀ *Love is the Greatest Spiritual Gift*—We hear in First Corinthians, Chapter 13, one of the most popular sections of Scripture, that love is greater than all of the other virtues. We have the text that proclaims: "Love is always patient and kind; it is never jealous; love is never boastful or conceited; it is never rude or selfish; it does not take offence and is not resentful...love does not come to an end. ... In short, there are three things that last: faith, hope, and love; and the greatest of these is love." We also hear in Paul's Letter to the Romans, Chapter 13, "All the Commandments are summed up in this single command: You must love your neighbor as yourself."

❀ *Love within the Community of Faith*—We find in John's Gospel that love is a reality that unites the relationship between Father, Son, and Spirit and also the relationship between God and God's people. During the Last Supper, Jesus' "Washing his disciples feet" is an active parable of love. In Chapter 13 of John's Gospel, we hear: "I give you a new Commandment: love one another; just as I have loved you, you must love one another." And in Chapter 15, we read: "As the Father has loved me, so I have loved you. Remain in my love. If you keep my Commandments, you will remain in my love, just as I have kept my Father's Commandments and remain in his love." And then further along in Chapter 15, we read, "This is my Commandment: love one another, as I have loved you. A man can have no greater love than to lay down his life for his friends." In addition to John's Gospel, we read in the First Letter of John that we need to focus on love for one another. "Anyone who loves his brother is living in the light. This has taught us love, that he gave up his life for us; and we, too, ought to give up our lives for our friends." In Chapter 4 of John's First Letter we read: "My dear people, let us love one another since love comes from God and everyone who lives love is begotten by God and knows God ...This is the love I mean: not our love for God, but God's love for us when he sent his son to be the sacrifice that takes our sins away." And, further along, "God is love and anyone who lives in love lives in God and God lives in him." And once more, "Anyone who says, I love God, and hates his brother is a liar, since the person who does not love the brother that he can see cannot love God, whom he has never seen."

The love command was central to Jesus' own message and mission. Love equals active goodwill toward the other; love also involves the whole person. It is more than "emotions" or "affections."

It would be impossible to read through the four Gospels and the Epistles, as well as the Letters of John, without recognizing that the fundamental Christian call is to love extensively. Since we have first been loved by God, we have a special obligation to love one another as a manifestation of our desire to love God.

The Ethic of Jesus

Jesus did not come primarily as an ethical teacher. In order to come to a conclusion about his ethical framework, we need to plumb the depths of the portraits we have in the rich prism of the four Gospels. On the basis of this evidence, we can reasonably lay out some of the central and common elements of the ethics that he preached.

* *The Coming of the Kingdom of God*—Jesus proclaimed a reality and issued a call. He asserted that the Kingdom of God is both present and not yet present. The day and hour in which it will be

brought to completion is not known. However, his disciples are to live as if it is coming soon. This gives a sense of urgency to our life in the world and encourages us to try to live consistently by the highest values of the Gospel.

❀ *The Demand for Conversion (Metanoia)*—John the Baptist, who prepared the way for the Lord, preached repentance for sins. Jesus gave a lot of attention to the theme of conversion. For example, in the 15th Chapter of Luke's Gospel, we have the three related parables of the Lost Sheep, the Lost Coin, and the Lost, or Prodigal, Son. In each of these stories we see that metaphorically God seeks out those who are lost. In addition, Jesus was a friend of publicans and sinners and shared table fellowship with them. Indeed, he did not live by the established Jewish standards of social engagement. He clearly attempted to speak the words of salvation to those who were written off by the leaders of the Jewish social order. Jesus also condemned the self-righteous and the presumptuous. We see this clearly in the Parable of the Pharisee and the Publican in the 18th Chapter of Luke's Gospel. Metanoia, or conversion, was a call to immediate decision-making by those who were attracted to his message. And we have examples in the Gospels of those who were instantaneously responsive and those who turned away.

❀ *The Demand for Faith*—The acceptance of a life of faith is the positive side of conversion. In Jesus' healing ministry, his miracle stories are almost always connected to a preexisting faith, which is manifest, or a call to faith by those who have been healed.

❀ *The Call to Discipleship*—The simplest expression of Jesus' outreach to those to whom he preached was "Come follow me." Some of Jesus' expressions of what was demanded seem rather excessive but they could surely capture the imaginations of those who listened to him preach. He encouraged them to leave everything, that is, family, house and farm, money and wealth, former occupations, and all economic security. We might call that discipleship to the nth degree. He also warned them that if they took this path they could expect hatred, suffering, persecution, and even death in response. That is why "Take up your cross and follow me" is at the heart of his message. We are encouraged, especially in light of the resurrection, to live lives in imitation of Christ.

❁ *The Great Commandment – Love of God and Neighbor*—We have versions of the Great Commandment in Mark's, Matthew's, and Luke's Gospels. Our call is to agape, or unconditional love. One manifestation of this is what has become called the Corporal Works of Mercy, which are laid out in Chapter 25 of Matthew's Gospel. This urges us to reach out in care and solicitude as we respond to the needs for food, drink, clothing, housing, accompaniment through sickness, visitation in jail, and proper Christian burial. Another expression of the same reality is Jesus washing the feet of his twelve Apostles at the Last Supper as seen in Chapter 13 of John's Gospel. The import of all of these texts is that we cannot genuinely manifest our love of God without also loving our neighbor in turn. These are integrally connected.

Jesus and the Social Order—Jesus, in the Gospels, is not presented as a social revolutionary. We see in one of his temptations in the desert, before he began his public ministry, that he was tempted to political Messiahship, but he rejected that option. Nevertheless, his disciples have a mission in the world, that is, to transform it. Despite the efforts of various theoreticians, the Gospels have no economic or political theory as such. Among other things, Jesus expresses an unusual openness toward women in his public ministry. He constantly reminds us that the standards of the Kingdom will often be just the opposite of those of the earthly realm. He speaks of the great reversal at the end of time when the first will be last and the last first. If nothing else, this can spark an important degree of humility for those of us who may know some degree of success and acclaim during our time in this life.

❁ *The Parables*—A parable is a metaphor or simile drawn from everyday life, arresting the hearer by its goodliness or strangeness and leaving the mind in significant doubt about its precise application to tease it into active thought. The Parables convey, in vivid story-like form, a number of dimensions of the Kingdom of God. For example, some speak of God's mercy for sinners. Others focus on the coming of God's Kingdom, which will triumph in the end over all alternative powers. Then, there is the importance of God's Judgment for all human beings in which how they have lived during their earthly lives will make all the difference. Jesus also speaks as if the end is near, which can be taken either literally or as a metaphor for a sense of urgency about making good moral decisions. He also encourages his disciples to be resolute in their actions. But most of all, his parables are about the love manifested in our lives as citizens of various communities, as well as in our relationships with our family members, our friends, and even our enemies. Jesus, who came as the Prince of Peace, intends for us to be agents of peace, harmony and reconciliation. When we do so, we are making love concrete.

❋ *The Example of Jesus*—Jesus not only provided an ethic for our reflection through his words and teaching, but also through his actions. He reached out across social, religious, and economic barriers. He formed a community of faith that was not only called to live in harmony with each other, but also to be agents for the transformation of the communities around it. He healed, he forgave sins, and, when necessary, was willing to face the political and religious powers of the day with great courage and bravery. Of course, the great irony is that the very people who put him to death on the cross never imagined that, after his resurrection from the dead and the gift of the Spirit at Pentecost, the community he founded would continue to be a force for good for millennia in the future.

The Christian Paradox

Every community needs stories to sustain its common life. We talk about heroic figures from the past and examples of individuals whose deeds and style of life continue to inspire us. In the Christian life, we tell stories of the great men and women whom we call saints because in one way or another they personified the Gospel. Thus, Mary the mother of Jesus, St. Paul the Apostle to the Gentiles, Francis of Assisi, Teresa of Avila, and more contemporary figures like Francis Xavier Cabrini, Andre Bessette, and Pope John XXIII are exemplars of the Gospel.

In a sense, saints are religious all-stars. They provide the power of example and deal with their successes with humility. They are the personification of giftedness in the power of the Holy Spirit.

In contrast, public sinners know the agony of defeat. They have, for whatever reason, failed to live by the values that they proclaim. As a result, either civil society or the Church community holds them accountable for their misdeeds. This does not mean that public sinners are abandoned but rather that they stand in stark contrast to the saints among us. Reprobates are those who try to change the rules to serve themselves. They often appear prosperous in the public eye, but have gained their preeminence by unsavory means. This is true not only of individuals who rob banks or engage in narcotics trafficking or kill people for money, but also those in the upper echelons who have taken advantage of the inability of individuals and groups to protect themselves from harm.

The Gospel and the teaching of Jesus reminds us constantly that we are always most properly judged in terms of our interior life rather than our public persona. In the end, the Christian paradox is that we are taught in the Gospel about the great reversal at the end of time, that those who are first in the world's eyes will be among the last and the last will be among the first. Those who are considered great in the Kingdom of God are those who have been the servants of the rest. At the end of one's life, it is not the fame that one has achieved or the economic success or the political power, but rather the legacy of dedicated service that one leaves behind. Worldly success does not last forever and it is our responsibility to seek to make a positive difference in the world, especially in light of those who carry the heaviest burden during their earthly existence. The Christian paradox is ultimately a very positive message for it gives all of us hope that, whatever our condition in life, we are beloved by God and that no set of temporary disadvantages can ever estrange us from the love and mercy of God.

The Resurrection of the Whole Person

Creatures of Flesh and Blood

Each of our bodily existences defines who we are in the world. Our physical appearance is co-relative with our identity. It is a manifestation of our uniqueness. This comes from, among other things, our face and our voice. Our five senses are our portals to the world—our mouth, nose, eyes, ears, and touch. Our major organs—brain, heart, lungs—are employed in terms of determining when we have ended our mortal existence. As creatures of flesh and blood we have bodily needs for food, drink, rest, and exercise. It is also the case that our bodily handicaps limit our capacity to be effective in the world. This would include sensory deprivations like blindness, deafness, inability to speak, lack of taste or tactility. We can also have corporal deprivations like immobility, attention deficit disorder, emotional distress, addictions, loss of memory, and verbal incoherence.

Creatures of Spirit

Our sense of uniqueness also comes from our inner identity like our name or our ID number. It is a function of self-awareness, self-knowledge, our level of maturity, and the distinctiveness of our personality. Our inner world is also defined by our personal history. As we grow older, we all have a story to tell. This includes our moral trajectory, our successes and failures in love, and in deeds of justice. We also are influenced by various significant others. And, for some of us, we have been through a conversion experience or a re-conversion. As creatures of spirit, we have spiritual needs for prayer, quiet, the sacraments, and a supportive community.

The Human Nature of Jesus

In Christian theology, we proclaim that Jesus was both fully human and fully divine. His utter humanity sprang from his physical reality. His appearance, intelligence, personality, sense of humor, agility, physical dexterity, and musical ability would all help to define who he was as a first-century Jewish person. Like all of us, Jesus had to go through various stages of development. He had to learn to crawl, walk, talk, and learn to love. He had to go through puberty and he had to learn various social skills. In these cases, we highlight the roles of Mary and Joseph in helping raise him to maturity. It is interesting that in various artistic representations of Jesus, the artists tend to imagine him as one of their ethnic and cultural group. Thus, we see in the classic images of the Madonna or the Crucifixion, or the Pieta, that Jesus and his contemporaries bear striking resemblance to people like ourselves.

Jesus' Healing Ministry

If we understand a miracle as an extraordinary event manifesting divine intervention in human affairs, we can see that Jesus performed signs and wonders as manifestations of the power of the Kingdom of God. They were intended to invoke faith or reinforce preexisting faith. When Jesus healed someone of leprosy, or deafness, or blindness, or some other physical limitation, he healed the whole person. Sometimes he was very explicit that, in healing some physical infirmity, he would also free the individual of his or her sin. But it needs to be remembered that all miracles were temporary cures since everyone would still eventually die.

Resurrection of the Body

It is a central tenet of Christian faith that Jesus rose from the dead as a whole person. He lived on in a transformed mode of life. When he made his appearances, as described in the various Gospels, he was not always instantaneously recognizable to his disciples. Sometimes he had to say something to them or share a meal with them, but eventually they came to recognize that he was the same Jesus that they had known in his lifetime. It is our faith and our hope that we too can enjoy a resurrection of our soul and physical body after which we will reign with Christ in eternal glory. This is our ultimate hope as a Christian person that death will not be the final word. All of us believers can look forward to the great banquet at the end of time when we will know love in its fullness in the presence of the Living Lord.

The Christmas Crèche

St. Francis of Assisi in the 13th Century was a major promoter of the Christmas crèche. Much of the worshiping population at that time was illiterate and it was commonplace in churches and cathedrals to have significant stained glass windows and paintings as a kind of catechesis. Many of the biblical stories could be interpreted simply by following along and looking at the windows and paintings, as well as the Stations of the Cross.

The utter simplicity of the Christmas crèche has always been part of its appeal. The basics are the images of the baby Jesus in the cradle with Mary and Joseph looking lovingly upon him. Normally it is seen as part of a manger place where animals are kept so that in the backdrop often are sheep and cattle and sometimes camels. More elaborate scenes may have other animals like dogs and cats. In addition to the Holy Family, there will also be shepherds and the three Magi, except sometimes the Magi are not added until the celebration of the Feast of the Epiphany. Other features would include angels and the Star of Bethlehem.

Having seen many crèche scenes throughout my life, especially on trips to other countries, it is clear that one of the most important elements is that Jesus, Mary, Joseph, and the other humans in the scene often resemble the people of that particular place or culture when it comes to race, ethnicity, and clothing. Just as portraits of Mary and Jesus as Madonna and child from around the world will resemble the people who are using it for worship and reflection, so it is with the crèche scene.

In contemporary American culture, with its pluralistic society and court interventions about the public display of religious symbols, it has become even more popular to have a crèche scene in front of churches, religiously affiliated schools and hospitals and in other places that are trying to celebrate the Christmas season in a religiously charged way. For example, on the Notre Dame campus, every hall chapel, almost all of the academic buildings and offices and many of the other public places have crèche scenes. In the Lady Chapel of Sacred Heart Basilica there is an especially popular, very beautiful version and another one outside, in the back, adjacent to the Grotto.

Theologically, Christmas always needs to be interpreted relative to Easter. The Nativity of the Lord is the great celebration of the full humanity of Jesus, like us in everything but sin, and Easter is the celebration of the fullness of his divinity. But we are reminded in a very concrete way at Christmastime of the important roles that Mary and Joseph played in protecting Jesus from harm and in accompanying him in the stages that every human person must go through from learning how to crawl and walk to learning how to talk and engage in social dynamics to learning how to pray according to the Jewish tradition. It is, of course, the heart of the great Christian mystery that at Christmas we celebrate God's great love for humanity by God being manifest in the baby Jesus in all of his vulnerability and precariousness. Every mother and every father should be able to relate to the scene from their own personal experience. And we are also reminded that each of us started with the same set of human needs that Jesus had in his birth in the manger.

Decalogue (The Ten Commandments)

Many Christian interpreters have seen the Decalogue or Ten Commandments as the basis of human morality, at least as a starting point. There are two main versions, one in Chapter 20 of Exodus and one in Chapter 5 of Deuteronomy. The texts depict a revelation by God on Mt. Sinai. It is God's covenant written on two tablets of stone. The present form of the Decalogue is traceable back to the 6th and 7th Centuries before the Christian era.

Many speculate that the number ten is really a mnemonic device corresponding to the ten fingers or ten toes on the human body. Different religious groups have different methods of counting which ones are the Commandments by number. But this is relatively unimportant. There is also speculation on theological grounds that the two tablets can be divided into the first three describing our proper relationship to God and the second seven describing our responsibility to other humans. The Commandments are seen as a kind of apodictic law which require no explanation.

Most of the Commandments start "You shall not... ." For the Jews, after the exile, the Law became the guide of life. All of this eventually morphed into the pharisees computing 613 distinct Commandments. Let me now go through the Commandments in turn.

❀ *"You shall have no gods except me. You shall not make yourself a carved image or likeness of anything in heaven or in earth beneath or in the waters under the earth."*

This Commandment decrees a practical monotheism and the proscription of images so that there can be no idolatry. When archeologists have dug up ancient Israelite cities they have found no images of Yahweh. During the history of Israel there were many other deities that the people and their unfaithfulness turned to, often the gods of their surrounding neighbors or conquerors. The prophets of Israel came along to remind the people that there was only one God, Yahweh, and that they needed to be faithful to the covenant with their God. In our own time in history, many gods offer themselves for our devotion—from money and land, to power and patriotism, to fame, fortune, and a libidinous lifestyle. All of us are tempted to worship false gods.

❀ *"You shall not utter the name of Yahweh your God to misuse it."*
Although many people in our contemporary world think of this
Commandment as referring to swearing and four-letter words
and other such things, in the biblical context it revolved primarily around forbidding the perjured use of the name of God.
The people were not to use curses or magic formulas to suggest
that they could control God rather than being obedient to God.
We can think in our time of various kinds of false prophets and
evil leaders usurping the authority of God. Some of these have
formed sectarian communities in which they totally control the
lives of their followers. Others have accumulated money, fame,
and public authority on the basis of their identifying their life
work and word with the living God.

❀ *"Remember the Sabbath day and keep it holy."*
It is often said that the great contribution of the Jews to all of humanity was the creation of the notion of the Sabbath. It breaks the
monotony and routine nature of the life of work and consecrates
a period of time to God. It is an opportunity for refreshment and
rest. We can use this time to recall the great things that God has
done for us. We interpret the Sabbath more flexibly in contemporary life, for example, with Catholics celebrating the Sabbath
liturgies from 4:00 p.m. on Saturday on through the conclusion of
Sunday. The business of contemporary life is a great temptation to
forsake the regular opportunity to worship with the community
of faith. For many, the weekend is full of other activities from kids'
sports to discretionary travel to hobbies and avocations. In the
biblical sense, God awaits our weekly presence.

❀ *"Honor your father and mother so that you may have a long life in
the land that Yahweh or God has given you."*
This Commandment seems to focus on the maintenance of
family life in general. For example, it would be appropriate
for the old and young in the family to recognize their mutual
responsibilities for each other since eventually the young will
become old themselves and will be more dependent on their own
children and grandchildren. This is not intended as a defense of
domineering parental styles of interaction with their children or
a heavy handedness in discipline. Instead, it encourages parents
and children to focus on what unites them and how dependent

they are on mutual love and patience and understanding.

❀ *"You shall not kill."*

At its face value, this protects the sacredness of human life by forbidding murder. In the end, life belongs to God. In the Israelite context, it also is a banning of blood feuds that often broke out. As we will know, Christians and other human beings have struggled with the application of this Commandment throughout human history. We have had to try to figure out when killing on behalf of the state or to protect the innocent or national sovereignty is allowable. We also have had to reflect about the sacredness of life in the womb and what is acceptable as far as interventions during the last stages in the dying process. The hardest questions of all have been wartime violence as well as capital punishment.

❀ *"You shall not commit adultery."*

Primarily, this Commandment protects the sanctity of marriage. It is a way of thinking about responsibilities of spouses for each other and also the inappropriateness of others pursuing a married person as a potential partner. But through much of human and Christian history, the whole area of sexuality and the various stages of human relationships have been in the forefront of reflection. Thus, we have disagreements about premarital, marital and post-marital sexual behavior and relationships. In the end, this Commandment is about the celebration of committed love.

❀ *"You shall not steal."*

In this Commandment, property is seen as an extension of the "self" of the owner. The theft of a person's property is in a sense a way of limiting their freedom in the world. Even more drastically, it forbids the stealing of someone's freedom in the act of enslavement. This would be the worst possible violation for a Jew.

In the contemporary world, this Commandment would apply to such a wide range of human practices that flow from avarice and greed and human selfishness that it would be hard to catalog them all. This would include stealing from one's neighbor and from other members of one's family as well as robbing various retail establishments or utilizing the internet to illegally pass funds from one account to another or utilizing unsavory practices to prey on the weak and defenseless.

❀ *"You shall not bear false witness against your neighbor."*
This Commandment forbids perjured testimony. It excludes any false statement damaging to one's neighbor. By extension, it has been taken to forbid lying in its various forms and levels of severity. It presumes a commitment to truthfulness on behalf of humans and their regular interaction. For some this may seem a trivial area of concern but it is fundamental to reliable social interaction of every kind. This will be true of the relationship between husbands and wives, parents and children, neighbors in the community, church members, and the broader national and human community.

❀ *"You shall not covet your neighbor's house nor your neighbor's wife or servants or his ox or his donkey or anything that is his."*
These two Commandments prohibit elicit desires. One should not engage in self-serving plots or intrigues. You can see this historically in the relationship between tribes or ethnic groups or clans of various kinds and, in contemporary society, it still exists in various nefarious formats.

The Ten Commandments are, in a sense, the beginning—a reflection about a universal framework for morality. They identify certain areas worthy of reflection and relate them all to our relationship to God. Subsequently, in human history, we have had many very sophisticated reflections about values, laws, and practices. And, in the Christian tradition, we have many texts from the New Testament that are significant in the ways that they clarify the nature of the moral life for a Christian person. These would include, of course, the Sermon on the Mount, the love Commandment and the parable about judgment at the end of time (in which we have one version of the corporal works of mercy). During the course of human and religious history, the Ten Commandments have been elaborated, reflected upon, and enhanced. That should not surprise us. But we can turn with confidence to the behaviors identified in the Commandments as a good start for fundamental moral reflection.

The Sabbath

In the Third of the Ten Commandments we hear that we should keep holy the Sabbath day. Many think that this was the greatest contribution of Judaism to world religions. Both Christianity and Islam follow the example of the Jews by identifying one day of the week as a holy day. For the Jews the Sabbath was an opportunity to look back and recall the great things that God had done and also to celebrate in prayer and ritual God's continued presence in their lives and the glorious future they had to look forward to. The Jews celebrate the Sabbath on Saturday, Christians on Sunday, and Muslims on Friday.

In addition to its religious significance, the notion of the Sabbath sets a day aside for rest and refreshment. It breaks into the endless cycle of work and allows for a period of renewal that otherwise would not exist.

We have inherited not only the notion of the celebration of the Sabbath but also the establishment of the weekend. For most of us, Saturday and Sunday are intended to be days off. It allows us the opportunity to gather together as members of the family and to engage in activities of one kind or another that simply are not possible during the regular workweek. In the absence of the Sabbath and the weekend, as well as periodic opportunities for vacation, we would all be in an endless rut of non-stop work. Perhaps, certain type A's or workaholics would welcome this. But it goes against the grain of our recognition of human nature and human need.

There have been many intrusions on the notion of the Sabbath in this country and in other parts of the Western world. At one time in the United States there were blue laws that prohibited most stores from opening on Sunday. That has all gone by the wayside over the course of time. As we have become more secularized, more and more people expect everything to be available seven days a week and that requires some people to work on the weekend as well as the regular workweek. Second, we have the expectation for family life in a certain strata of society that there need to be endless opportunities for participation in sports and cultural activities. This puts strains on parents who are trying to do right for their kids. As this has gone from one extreme to another, it has meant for some parents and children that they spend the whole weekend going from one supervised event to the other. Sometimes, this does not allow a chance for worship or much time for simply enjoying one another's company. Third, some employers have eaten into the notion of both the weekend and the Sabbath in order to expect seven days of performance. This allows no real life or mode of relaxation for those who are employed in these kinds of circumstances. Sometimes the owner or founder of a company will use his or her own example in terms of what they expect from their employees. One of the great benefits of the Union Movement has been to try to protect workers from their employers when it comes to such demands. Finally, there are activities that of their very nature require some form of seven-day-a-week activity, like farming, restaurants, hospitals, police and firefighting work, and other forms of employment that are critical for the common well-being. The same is true of the military.

All of this means that the gift of the Sabbath has been slowly eroded over time. In the Catholic tradition we have expanded a number of opportunities of worship from Saturday after 4:00 p.m. through Sunday night. This allows for more convenient chances to worship according to one's personal schedule but it also does entail a high level of activity by clergy and lay ministers in parish settings. One does not have to be a hard-liner in terms of a kind of pure celebration of the Sabbath but it is important to recognize what a great gift it has been and how perilous our preservation of such a tradition can be. Not only do we need to pause and give thanks to God but we also need a chance to rest, relax and get a perspective on our lives. It is often a real plus to have periods

of quiet and unhurried paces of involvement in the day in order to be able to go through the cycles of life in a healthy and
successful way.

The Sabbath is a great gift of the Jews to humanity. May we
continue to protect it and the related notion of the weekend for
the common good.

Prophecy

In religious terms, a tradition of prophecy begins in Judaism,
especially in the period between 800 and 500 B.C. As Israel
discovered during its history, there were both authentic and in-
authentic prophets. An essential characteristic was that they
were called by Yahweh and their activity did not come from their
own initiative. In order to suggest this, each of the three major
prophets describes an event in which their prophetic call was
manifest. For Isaiah, it took the form of the purification of his
lips by fire. For Jeremiah, it was the experience of having words
put into his mouth. For Ezekiel, it was the eating of a sacred
scroll. Prophets were destined for a hard and lonely life. By
background, they came from all walks of life. For example, some
were shepherds, others farmers, and others nobles. Some forms of
prophecy were institutionalized and others were not. For example,
the ecstatic prophets functioned as the inspirers of troops going
off into battle. The cultic prophets engaged in intercessory prayer
around the major shrines. But the classic prophets of Israel could
not be circumscribed in this way. They appear without warning
and their message was validated only with the passage of time.

Much of the message of the prophets revolved around the
violation of the laws of the Torah. They condemned particular evils
like oppression, violence, debauchery, greed, theft, dishonesty, lust
for power, the callousness of humanity, and the lack of faithfulness to trust. It is surprising that they were not killed, but much

of their protection came from the recognition that they played a crucial role in preserving the distinctiveness of Israel's religious life. It could be said that the classic prophets of Israel were social revolutionaries but religious conservatives.

After the exile in Babylon, prophecy gradually lapsed. That is why the main New Testament prophetic figure is John the Baptist. It is interesting that the title "prophet" is never applied to Jesus explicitly, either by himself or by the evangelists. We hear in the Acts of the Apostles and in the Letters of Paul about the gift of prophecy in the New Testament community, but we are not sure how it functioned. In the post-apostolic communities, prophecy was claimed almost exclusively by heretical sects.

Etymologically, the word "prophet" in Greek refers to one who speaks for another. In Hebrew, it is the one who communicates the divine will.

There were various forms of prophetic communication. Most took place orally and we see that the great prophets of Israel spoke their messages. The sayings were then memorized by their disciples who gradually put them together and books were produced in their name. The style of the message of the prophets is always in the first person, that is, 'The Lord God says...." Typically, they use color and lavish imagery to grab the attention of their audiences. Often hyperbole characterized what they were about. In the final analysis, we can say that they employed all the tricks of orators.

In addition to their oral message and their distinctive style of communication, the prophets communicated by their concrete actions. For example, Isaiah walks naked as a sign of the eventual captivity of the people. Jeremiah places a loincloth in a hole where it will rot as a sign of the corruption of the people. Jeremiah also breaks an earthenware jar in public as a sign of the coming destruction. And Ezekiel uses a brick as a sign of the besieged city that is to come.

The prophets also communicated by their manner of life. For example, Jeremiah remains celibate as a sign of his coming death. Ezekiel engages in no mourning at the death of his wife. And Hosea forgives the sins of his adulterous wife, Gomer.

The prophetic sense of time is primarily focused on the present, that is, what is sinful needs to be opposed in the present scheme of things. Their predictions about the future are extrapolations from the moral and religious decline that they condemn. The great prophets of Israel criticize the chief beneficiaries of the existing system. This included kings and the way they exercised their authority, fat priests, greedy professional prophets who were their opponents, parasitic seers, those who live in luxury, venal judges, heartless creditors, and greedy land owners.

There are two significant minor prophets of Israel, Amos and Hosea. Amos is often seen as the prophet of social justice. He preached in a time of prosperity in the northern kingdom and spoke against materialism; oppression of the poor; widows and orphans; bribery; religious apostasy; and pagan worship. Although he predicted the "Day of the Lord" in which the Assyrians would crush the northern kingdom, he also promised a saving remnant, "which assured that some would survive to carry on the religious heritage." The second, Hosea, contrasted human infidelity with God's fidelity. In forgiving his adulterous wife, he manifested the way the people should live if they wanted to be welcomed back by God themselves. He assured them that super-power alliances would never save them.

The three major prophets of Israel were Isaiah, Jeremiah, and Ezekiel. Among the major themes of Isaiah were: monotheism—that God is one, holy, creator and master of us all; judgment—that God will punish sinful indulgence; and promise—that the Messiah will initiate a kingdom of justice and peace. Jeremiah, the second of the great prophets, is the longest book in the Bible. His message is often depressing. In English, a "Jeremiad" is a prolonged lamentation or complaint. He focused on themes like "national guilt," the "new covenant," and the "plague of false prophecy." The last of the great prophets, Ezekiel, yearns for a restoration of Israel. He wrote when they were in captivity in Babylon. His message is full of visions, raptures, symbolic actions, and allegories. While he predicted the destruction of Jerusalem, he also imagined its restoration. He stressed the need for the interior conversion of each person.

From our vantage point in history, we have much to learn from the tradition of the prophets of Israel. We need to be open to the genuine, God-given, messages that apply to the evils of our own day. We need to keep alive the sense of the connection between private morality and public morality. And, finally, we need to see that the condition of present-day society has built into it the seeds of either a bright or a depressing future.

THEOLOGICAL REFLECTIONS

The Roman Catholic tradition is rich with the contributions of a wide variety of individuals across two millennia of human history in order to apply the Hebrew and Christian Scriptures to the challenges of everyday life in the world. This is, indeed, faith-seeking understanding. In this section, I engage in a series of such reflections.

The Saints

The word saint comes from the Latin *Sanctus,* which means "holy one." In the New Testament, the word is used as a synonym for "Christian" and later was restricted to outstanding Christians. We can think of saints as heroines, exemplars, models, intercessors, protectors, and manifestations of God's power. In religious terms, a saint has been grasped by a religious vision that radically changes the kind of person they are and leaves others to admire the values that guide their lives.

One of the ways that we can recognize saints is to look at the martyrs. These were witnesses for the faith. It was because of the Roman persecutions that the cult of the saints began. Liturgical celebrations were held to mark the anniversaries of the death of martyrs, that is, the day when they were reborn as saints. During the time of persecution, Mass was celebrated on top of their relics that were built into the altars.

Another group of saints are called "confessors." These are

people who openly professed their faith but never were executed. Many of their oral testimonies have been subsequently published.

Saints often have simply been proclaimed by popular opinion. Sometimes, there were local cults celebrating men and women who were especially admired in their particular geographical area.

Eventually, the Church established a certain set of procedures for the formal canonization of a saint. This was partially to get greater control over who was celebrated, and insofar as possible, eliminate legendary elements. In the Thirteenth Century, Pope Gregory IX reserved the right of canonization to the papacy alone. However, the actual process was entrusted to one of the offices in the Vatican. In the Seventeenth Century, a full canonization process was introduced. Today, the formal proclamation of those to be recognized as saints is entrusted to a sacred congregation in the Vatican. The process begins by inquiry by a local bishop and a report being sent to Rome. Then there are individuals in the congregation given this responsibility entrusted to look at the positive and negative reports that have been received. The declaration of "beatification" is possible after two miracles have been accepted. This allows the pope to approve public veneration in the local church. Normally "canonization" requires four miracles (except for martyrs). The pope then officially declares the person to be a saint and the cult is extended to the whole Church. The relics of these individuals are then honored and the name is allowed to be included in the liturgical calendar. Most saints are not normally celebrated during the liturgical year, except in particular places. Pope John Paul II simplified the process to some extent and was responsible for the largest number of saints ever declared in one papacy. Pope Francis seems to be inclined in the same direction.

There have been a number of criticisms of the canonization process in recent history. Most saints in the calendar have been priests, nuns, and founders of religious communities. There were few married people, blue-collar workers or professionals. This has been improved in recent years by the addition of saints representing a broader cross-section of the Church community. Another criticism is that there has been an undue stress on doctrinal orthodoxy. Until recently, most saints have been Western European. This, fortunately, is changing rather drastically. On most occasions canonization is a slow and cumbersome process. In recent years, some have been concerned about the attempt to canonize all of the recent popes without much passage of time. It remains important that the saints of the past who have been proven to be legendary be expunged from the liturgical calendar.

In my eyes, it is appropriate for the Church to celebrate the lives and example of individuals who have been extraordinary in living out the Gospel. It is the primary Christian call from our baptism to seek to be holy. We are encouraged in the words of Jesus: "To be perfect as our heavenly Father is perfect." The saints can inspire us or cause us to reevaluate our lifestyle and value system and to seek to become the personification of the best Christian values. To claim that there have been saints in the world and saints in our own communities today is to recognize the power of the Holy Spirit to sanctify and transform all of us who claim to be his followers.

In addition to the prizing of relics of saints, the tradition of pilgrimages has always had an important function in the life of the Christian Catholic community. Those of us who are members of the Congregation of Holy Cross naturally wish to visit the St. Joseph Oratory in Montreal where St. André Bessette, C.S.C., carried on his ministry or Le Mans, France, where blessed Basil Moreau, our founder, lived and sent off members of our community to different parts of the world.

Some particular saints will have more attraction to each of us in turn than others. We may like that they represent some professional area of activity or be a member of our racial or ethnic group, or be someone who came from or served in our own geographical area. In human terms, saints were not perfect. What we celebrate is one particular virtue that they possessed to the nth degree. We then tolerate some of their personality quirks as relatively insignificant in the long run.

Among the most popular saints are, of course, the Blessed Virgin Mary, St. Peter, and St. Paul. These all played a decisive role in the Gospels and Epistles of the Christian Scriptures. Then there are outstanding leaders and thinkers like St. Augustine of Hippo, St. Thomas Aquinas, St. Dominic, and St. Ignatius of Loyola. There are saints also who have been paired together because of their common work, like St. Francis of Assisi and St. Clare, St. Vincent de Paul and St. Louise de Marillac, St. Martin de Porres and St. Rose of Lima, St. Teresa of Avila and St. John of the Cross, St. Jane Chantal and St. Francis de Sales. Some saints are honored in a special way in certain countries like St. Patrick in Ireland, the Uganda martyrs, St. Albert the Great in Germany, and the North American martyrs. There are women saints to have special recognition like St. Joan of Arc, St. Thérèse of Lisieux, St. Bridget of Sweden, St. Margaret of Scotland and St. Catherine of Siena. Some saints are honored for what seems are peculiar reasons like St. Jude (the patron of hopeless cases), St. Anthony De Padua (the finder of lost things), St. Blaise (the blessing of throats), St. Nicholas (the origin of Santa Claus), and St. Valentine (patron of lovers).

We honor collectively all of the saints canonized by the Church on All Saints Day, November 1st. These are the holy men and women who have gone before us in the life of faith and we yearn for the day when we can be reunited with them in the eternal banquet that Christ promises to those who love him.

Love and Christian Theology

As Christians have reflected about the priority of love in the Christian Scriptures, this has led them to draw upon a wide range of sources to help clarify what this might entail. There is a long tradition of using a series of Greek terms to talk about the different forms of love. These include:

- ❧ *Epithemia* equals "lust." In this early sense, love can be seen as a kind of over-mastering desire or bodily appetite. It is one way of understanding how sexual desire functions for the human person as he or she moves into adulthood. At this level, love is more a drive that comes from our make-up as human beings than the later manifestations of love.

- ❧ *Eros* equals "love of the good, true, and beautiful." Love as *eros* means that we recognize that we have appetites and a yearning desire that is aroused by the attractive qualities of its object. *Eros* tends to be acquisitive and egocentric. It wants to possess the person loved. Historically, certain symbols of *eros* have been provided by theologians and poets including the heavenly ladder, the wings of the soul, the ascent of the mountain, the arrow, the flame, and the chain of love.

- ❧ *Philia* equals "friendship." *Philia* is love as preferential. It means that we share this level of love with only a few. Different people have a different level of capacity for friendship. In this sense, love is always exclusive but not necessarily exclusivistic. Friendship can also be seen as reciprocal love, the kind that we need to give and to receive. It is best done by free and equal participants. It includes both benevolence and the sharing of affections. Friendship always faces the problem of fidelity. As we grow older, our former friendships sometimes decline and are subject to change. Certain friendships in our lives simply cease. True friendship we know implicitly should be a relation of deep intimacy and concomitant loyalty. As we grow older, we discover that we need to work at friendship. It requires time and reinforcement. The other activities of our life can distract and preoccupy us. In this sense, all of us are subject to not having enough time left over for some of the fundamental relationships of our lives.

❀ *Agape* equals "self-sacrificial love." This highest level of love that we call *agape* involves whole-hearted surrender to God. It has a kind of universal or all-embracing quality to it. It is freely given and freely received. It also has the capacity of forgiveness for offenses committed by the one we love. It arises often spontaneously and without motivation. In the end, it is unconditional love. This is the kind of manifestation of love we see in the life of Jesus as well as in that of the great saints of human history, especially the martyrs.

Having looked at these different manifestations or levels of love, it is important to think about what love requires. Only human persons are capable of this kind of love. For most people it involves the utilization of words, gestures, and bodily expression. Sexual intercourse, in the right context, is, in this world, one of the highest expressions of love that human beings can experience.

We learn love by receiving it, by practicing it, and by participating in loving communities. That is why family life is so important as well as being involved in nurturing communities. At its best, the Church needs to be a primary community of love.

We can ask why love is so important. The answer is that it is the primary Christian call because God has first taken up the initiative and Jesus has revealed that the very nature of God is a love among three persons. Love also promotes human happiness and it creates human bondedness.

For most human persons love and sexuality are inevitably connected. Sexuality is present in all human relations. Pleasure given and received can express love profoundly, but it need not. Pleasurable sexual expression has the potential to speak eloquently as shared between lovers who are friends. *Agape* and *eros* interpenetrate in committed, mature relationships. We can say as human persons living in the world that God is known in loving the other person.

Prayer and the Moral Life

For a Christian believer, participation in the life of prayer is both an opportunity and a necessity. It allows us to keep rooted in the God who brought us into existence, who nourished us through the power of the spirit, and who yearns to welcome us home to eternal life. A simple definition of prayer is a conversation with God. We know from the Scriptures and from Christian theology that God is always attentive to each of us as individuals and that he knows us each by name. He never tunes us out or affects an attitude of indifference to our situation. On the other hand, it is more challenging for us to be in conversation with someone we cannot see directly. That is why the practices of prayer, like the Sacraments, are opportunities for us to listen to the Word of God, to respond to its call, and to achieve a greater sense of God's presence in our lives.

While prayer is essential for the Christian life in general, it is also crucial for good moral decision-making. Through our intelligence and human freedom, we have many opportunities to choose well instead of poorly, to enhance our dignity as a human person, and to be of assistance to people in need. In trying to live a virtuous life, we can draw upon our previous experience and what we have learned from the example of the holy men and women who have gone before us in the life of faith.

I think there are certain qualities that flow from the commitment of the whole self to prayer that can affect moral decision-making. First, we need a sense of confidence in God's benevolence. God is on our side. God is not out to get us. God understands the perplexity under which we sometimes have to make choices. If we strive to do our best and have given ourselves enough time for proper reflection, we can simply trust that God will understand when everything does not turn out exactly as we hoped.

Second, moral decision-making can be improved in prayer by

recognition of the ambiguity of appearances. The world is sometimes opaque, so sometimes we are faced with decisions that have no clear answer. In prayer, we can try to get to the heart of the matter, to dispel the clouds that obscure what is really going on. Sometimes our motives might be mixed and we may see that as an obstacle. And yet, that is the way we are made as human persons and we need to strive for the best intentions possible under the circumstances.

Third, prayer can cultivate in us an attitude of social interdependence. We are never entirely alone, either in our relationship to God or in our relationship to our family members, friends, companions, and the fullness of humanity. In times of grief, or failure, or disappointment, our spirits can often be buoyed by the presence of others who abide with us even when things do not go right. Reciprocally, we can do the same for others so that we continue to reinforce our sense of family, community and Church.

Finally, prayer can give us a sense of patience with the rhythms of life. Each of the stages of development as a person will have different levels of responsibility. A grade-school kid and a teenager live in a different moral universe in many ways from the father or mother of a family, a parent, a grandparent, a civic leader, or someone who runs a business. It will be easier to have confidence in moral decision-making at each stage of our life when we have incorporated practices of prayer into it. My predecessor as President of Notre Dame, Fr. Ted Hesburgh, C.S.C., used to recommend to people who came to him for counsel that when they faced a difficult decision of whatever kind they should simply pray, "Come Holy Spirit." They could then be confident that they had available to them the very best assistance possible. Good habits of prayer are an acknowledgement that in our moral decision-making we are never operating alone. We will always have available to us the inspiration of the Holy Spirit and the assistance of trusted advisors. This puts us at a great advantage over others who may think that they are completely isolated and need to make decisions alone.

The Sacrament of Penance

It is clear from the scriptural evidence that Jesus himself forgave the sins of others. In Chapter 2 of Mark, he forgives the sins of the paralytic whom he had cured. In Chapter 7 of Luke, he forgives the sins of the woman who anoints his feet. It also seems clear that Jesus confers on Peter and the other disciples the power of "binding and loosing." In one of his post-resurrection appearances, in Chapter 20 of John, he says to the Apostles, "Receive the Holy Spirit. Those whose sins you forgive are forgiven..." There is no direct and undisputed evidence that Jesus himself established a sacramental form for penance. Instead, it evolved in the history of the Church.

In the early Church there seems to have been a presumption that adult converts would never sin seriously again. This was called into question by a crisis in the time of persecution in the Third Century. One heretical group called the Montanists, represented by Tertullian, taught that only the Church can forgive sins, but it should not, lest others also commit sins. The contrary position was taken by Cyprian, who encouraged tolerance toward those who had lapsed (that is, sacrificed to idols), during the time of persecution.

By the time of the Post-Constantinian Church, that is, between the Fourth and Sixth Centuries, there had developed a structure of public penance. It was seen to be exceptional, public, dramatic, involving a laborious penance, and having severe after-effects. This public penance was designated for a triad of sins, including murder, adultery, and apostasy. It could be participated in only once in a lifetime. The bishop was the primary celebrant, except in situations of emergency. As a result of the severity of the impact on one's life, people tended to put off participation in the sacrament until their deathbed.

Between the Seventh and the Thirteenth Centuries, there developed a structure of frequent, private penance. On the continent, it was seen as a means of moral catechesis. Because many of the confessors had a limited theological background, there developed the so-called "penitential books." This allowed for uniformity of participation by providing guidance for clergy who were generally relatively uneducated. There was also some evidence that the practice of lay confession took place, that is, friend-to-friend. It included correction, encouragement, and some assignment of a penance.

In 1215, at the Fourth Lateran Council, the Church imposed an annual confession on those who have sinned gravely in preparation for their obligatory Easter communion. At this time in history, there was a debate among scholastic theologians about what the proper attitude should be for a worthy participation in the sacrament. A more severe position argued for "contrition," which required hatred of sin, love of God, and a resolution not to sin again. The other position was called "attrition," or imperfect sorrow. The fear of hell could be seen as sufficient interior disposition. In response to this debate, the Council asserted that the purpose of amendment should be firm, efficacious and universal. In some cases, absolution could be delayed until some deed was performed—for example, to finish a pilgrimage to some sacred place.

With the coming of the Protestant Reformation, the debate about whether penance was a sacrament became one of the critical points. In Martin Luther's early writings, he accepted penance as a sacrament, but later, on biblical grounds he rejected it. John Calvin thought of penance as unscriptural and therefore would not accept it as a sacrament. In the Sixteenth Century, in response to the Protestant Reformation, the Council of Trent focused on a number of elements connected to the sacrament of penance. It required that the number, species, and circumstances of a particular sin should be an integral part of confession. In addition, the priest must say "I absolve you...." The effects of the sacrament were said to be reconciliation with God, forgiveness of sins, revival of merits, and forgiveness of venial sins. The Council also bound the bishop or priest to secrecy. It also taught that the fear of punishment could be a sufficient inner disposition for a worthy confession.

In the Eastern Orthodox Churches, confession is not frequent. It is linked with Holy Communion and there is a stress on a sorrowful heart rather than the details of sins. Roman Catholic practice with regard to the Sacrament of Penance (or Reconciliation) has changed rather dramatically in the post-Vatican II Church. For many Catholics who grew up in a previous generation, the central issue is "why" not "how." As a result, in many parts of the country and world, Catholics participate less frequently in the sacrament, sometimes going years without being involved. In the wake of the Council, a number of people have written about how their experiences with particular priests or preoccupation with certain sins has left them dissatisfied. In many places, the younger generation is unaccustomed to regular participation in Reconciliation.

One point of contention has to do with the distinction between mortal and venial sin. There have been intense debates about the nature of sin, the degree of personal freedom necessary to be alienated totally from God, and what types of sins in one's life should receive the most attention. For example, as a confessor one can say that many Catholics are prone to confess primarily sins that have to do with sexuality. It is much less common to have people focus on matters like the place of wealth in their lives or their participation in or support of acts of violence, or various kinds of societal judgmentalism. One of the challenges to the Church today is to give an effective catechesis of sin so that, when people are reviewing their moral life and seeking a sacramental opportunity to bring that reality to the sacrament to be forgiven, they need much more catechesis than was available earlier in their moral formation. Another question has to do with the recognition that the Eucharist is the prime sacrament of forgiveness. That is why, at the beginning of every Mass, we confess our sins and receive forgiveness from the priest. Finally, the decline in the number of priests in many parts of the country and world have made the necessity of priests for a valid sacrament more problematic.

Today we have in most churches an area set aside for participation in the sacrament of Reconciliation. People have two options, that is, to remain anonymous behind a screen or to have a face-to-face conversation with a confessor. There are also celebrations of communal reconciliation in which, on occasion, a number of priests from the outside are brought in so that there can be both a common reflection and the opportunity for private confession as well.

There are a number of lingering issues as we move forward. One is the matter of whether it is preferable to preserve anonymity or not. Especially when there is only one priest assigned to a given church, some people may be hesitant to come before the priest who would recognize them either by their appearance or by their voice. Then there is the matter of gender since it seems from their own reflections that women are often hesitant to bring some of their primary concerns before a male confessor. In some places where confession is made regularly available with multiple celebrants, like at the University of Notre Dame, many participants seem more in need of religious counseling than sacramental forgiveness. Often they are quite pious and highly motivated to live the fullness of the Christian life. But sometimes they suffer from different levels of scrupulosity. Finally, there is the matter of the age of first confession and the experience that children have in the sacrament. Most of us know from our own experience that the early experience of children with the sacrament can have a profound impact on their later levels of participation. That is why Pope Francis' message to priest/confessors to be agents of God's mercy is well taken.

In thinking about the future of penance in the Catholic tradition, it is worth reflecting about Protestant practice today. On one hand, we have the tradition of "the Revival," which intended to be a vivid personal experience of Jesus as Lord and Savior (usually accompanied by stories of one's life of sin). This seems to be intended as a once and for all moment of conversion. And yet, many people have gone through testifying to their conversion at multiple revivals. There is also in the Charismatic tradition the laying on of hands and healing directed towards sinners. Finally, there is the kind of hellfire-and-brimstone preaching that is intended to in a sense scare people into an amendment of their lives.

That there remains sin in the world and that human beings are tempted to various types of sins during the course of their lives is manifestly clear. But the Church has gone through various stages in developing rituals and sacramental forms to help people to experience the grace of God's forgiveness in their lives. The ultimate Christian message of mercy and forgiveness has more to do with the disposition of one's innermost self than with a rigorous cataloging of every failure. Jesus' words to the public sinners brought to him for correction are applicable to us as well: "Go in peace, and sin no more."

Church Leadership

St. Peter, the Apostle, is recognized as the leader among the Apostles and was the first Pope. He was flawed in some dramatic ways, including denying the Lord three times after his arrest and displaying an excessive self-confidence several times during Jesus' public ministry. But in John's Gospel, he is instructed to tend the sheep of the Lord and to feed them. Peter was faithful until the end and, after Pentecost, was courageous in preaching the Gospel. By tradition, he was crucified upside down on a cross in Rome and buried underneath what is now the main altar of St. Peter's Cathedral.

In the course of its history, the Church has had saintly and outstanding leaders as well as those who were public sinners and relatively inept in proclaiming the Gospel. There was also a period when there were contenders for who the real Pope was and at one time there were three different rivals. The closer we come to contemporary time, the more the role of the papal office has been accentuated. From the first Vatican Council on, it has been recognized that certain powers accrue to the one who holds the papal office.

In my lifetime, I have seen seven different popes. Each was different by personality and by the style of leadership that they provided. John the XXIII brought *aggiornamento* to the Church, a kind of openness of spirit in which all things could be reviewed and renewed. This led to the calling of the Second Vatican Council and the issuing of several social encyclicals. Paul VI completed the work of Vatican II. He was the first world traveler as Pope and reached out across various boundaries. He was also instrumental in asking Fr. Ted Hesburgh to establish what became the Tantur Ecumenical Institute. Some saw Paul VI as Hamlet-like, torn relative to some of the big decisions he had to make. John Paul I was Pope for such a short period of time that we hardly knew him. John Paul II was one of the longest-lived popes in Church history. He was a scholar, an actor, and an ardent anti-communist on the basis of his experience in Poland. He too was a world traveler, far exceeding the initial attempts of Paul VI. He was also a prolific saint maker, trying to have saints that represented the broad spectrum of humanity. Benedict was even more of a scholar by background and tradition than John Paul II. He was somewhat shy, but particularly fearful of secular culture. Francis is the first Jesuit Pope and he took Francis of Assisi as his model, thus the name. He is a master of symbolic gestures and many of these have captured the imagination of people outside of the Church community. He has worked hard at reforming the Vatican bureaucracy. He has also proclaimed a year of mercy and sent his emissaries around the world as agents of this outreach. He is a person with a big smile and a ready welcome who personifies the open arms that would characterize his view of the Church. He can also make all of us slightly uncomfortable with a smile and a word that calls us into account in terms of our priorities and lifestyles.

The individuals who have been called to serve as popes have had a very difficult set of responsibilities. On one hand, they do not want to become prisoners of the Vatican and its bureaucracy and, on the other hand, they want to proclaim the Gospel to as many of the segments of the Church community around the world as possible. This entails finding a core group of central advisors that one has confidence in who can attend to the daily matters that accrue to the office. It also requires a tough constitution so that one can deal with all of the hoopla and crowds and poignant moments that take place when the Pope is traveling. In our time, all of the popes have been seen as holy men. Several have already been canonized as Saints of the Church. We can be thankful to God that they were willing to take on this challenging task, relying as they did upon the Holy Spirit to guide them and to give them a sense of what they were being called to represent.

One of my favorite Church leaders in my lifetime has been Fr. Ted Hesburgh. He was not only my predecessor as President of Notre Dame, but a good friend as well. Fr. Ted was a visionary, a polyglot, and a polymath, full of endless energy. He was also quite resilient. He did not let the troubles of one day carry into the next. He too was a world traveler and told me one time that he had visited over 100 countries. But most of all he wanted to be remembered as a priest for whom the celebration of the Eucharist was primary. He was quite comfortable with non-Catholics and non-Christians and this was part of his allure as a Catholic leader.

Among the challenges that I think Church leaders of today have to take on are the following:

- Proclaim the Gospel of Jesus Christ with energy, faithfulness and enthusiasm;
- Establish and reinforce the community of faith (this means bringing together the sometimes divided Church communities that are split on often superficial grounds);
- Rely on the Holy Spirit for the power of renewal;
- Strive to be both humble and forthright; and
- Yearn for the eternal banquet when all will be brought to completion, which will be a fitting reminder that, in this world, in the end we have to leave all things in God's hands.

St. Thomas à Becket and St. Thomas More

Thomas à Becket was born in the 12th Century. He was smart, personable and ambitious. Eventually he studied law and became Chancellor of England.

King Henry II and he got into a dispute about the authority of the papacy relative to British governance. As a result, Thomas went into exile in France for a number of years. Eventually he became Archbishop of Canterbury, which was a very significant post of Church leadership. In this new role, he became much more alert to the prerogatives of the Catholic Church.

At a certain point, Henry II was quoted as saying, "Will no one rid me of this troublesome priest." This is referenced in T.S. Elliott's play *Murder in the Cathedral.* Thomas à 'Becket knew that his situation had become precarious. In Elliott's play he is quoted as saying (about one of his contemporaries), "The last temptation is the greatest treason; to do the right deed for the wrong reason." This was reference to the temptation to seek martyrdom for earthly glory and revenge.

Several knights, thinking they were implementing the will of Henry II, put Thomas à Becket to death in Canterbury Cathedral. He was quoted as saying, "I accept death for the name of Jesus and for the Church."

Soon after his death, Thomas à Becket was proclaimed a Saint of the Church. Canterbury became a place of great pilgrimage, as seen in Chaucer's *Canterbury Tales*.

Another great martyr and leader in British society was Thomas More. Thomas More died in the early part of the 16th Century, some four centuries after St. Thomas à Becket. He was a legal scholar, an author, and a married man with several children. He became the trusted advisor of King Henry VIII and was held in high regard by his contemporaries.

When Henry the VIII wanted to remarry after divorce, he created a situation of conscience for Thomas More. He did every-thing he could to try to find a compromise solution in the bitter dispute between Henry VIII and the pope of the time. All of this is captured well in Robert Bolt's play *A Man for All Seasons*.

In the play, at a critical moment when Richard Ridge had just been appointed by Cromwell as Attorney General of Wales, Thomas More says to him, "Why, Richard, it profits a man nothing to give his soul for the whole world...but for Wales!" In a sense, Thomas was acting out in his conversations with Richard Ridge what would become his own dilemma.

After a trial in Lambeth Palace and a long period of imprison-ment in London Tower, Thomas More was finally put to death by

King Henry VIII. In the Bolt play, he is quoted as saying, "I die the King's good servant, but God's first."

Thomas à Becket and Thomas More are both martyr saints who can stand as good models for those who exercise administrative responsibility both in society and in the Church. They were people of conscience who, in the end, chose to live by the highest values and not to succumb to peer pressure or offers of earthly reward.

Vocation

To have a vocation is to be called. For example, Israel understood itself as the chosen people of God. They were elected by Yahweh as a people of the covenant. This call as described in the Hebrew Scriptures was first made to Abraham and then repeated to Isaac and Jacob. Later on in Jewish history, Moses led the people of Israel to the Promised Land. There, under the leadership of Kings Saul, David, and Solomon, they became an established nation and prospered.

The prophets of Israel also experienced a calling. They asserted that their message was not of human initiative. This is described in the Scriptures in the following way: Isaiah describes a purification of his lips; Jeremiah describes the putting of words into his mouth; Ezekiel is pictured as eating a scroll. Each of these images is intended to convey that the words they proclaim came directly from Yahweh or God. Later on, at the beginning of the Christian Scriptures, John the Baptist, the last and the greatest of the prophets, is pictured as having a distinct call from God. And, when Jesus is baptized by John in the Jordan River, his call is manifest by the symbolic presence of the Father and the Holy Spirit.

In the New Testament the annunciation to Mary, the mother of Jesus, that she will become the mother of God is a primordial calling of a person to play a distinctive role in sacred history. The Angel Gabriel proclaims to her, "Rejoice so highly favored, the Lord is with you." Then later on, "Do not be afraid, you have won God's favor... you are to conceive and bear a son, and you must name him Jesus." Mary says in response, "I am the handmaid of the Lord, may what you have said be done to me." In religious terms Mary's yes to the call of God is one of the defining moments of history.

We have ten different accounts in the Christian Scriptures of the calls of the twelve Apostles. In each case, Jesus comes up to those to be called and in a sense, out of the blue, invites them to be his disciples. They were chosen not because of their manifest credentials or their particular set of pre-existing skills, but rather because they would, in faith, be charged with doing great things as proclaimers of the Gospel of the Lord. The Apostle Paul, later in history, describes his call in a dramatic way on the road to Damascus. The persecutor of the Christian community had become an Apostle. Eventually he was accepted by the Church in Antioch and ended up visiting with Peter and Paul in Jerusalem to receive approbation for the method by which Gentiles could become Christians.

Other classic Christian calls include:

- Augustine of Hippo—In his *Confessions* he describes his sense that he had a call to pick up and read the Gospel in the garden and this became the defining moment in his process of conversion.

- Francis of Assisi—He went from being a soldier to suffering injury, to becoming a hermit, to becoming a preacher of the ways of penance and poverty and the founder of a religious community.

- Ignatius of Loyola—He was injured in war. While he was recuperating, he read the lives of the saints, and then wrote the *Spiritual Exercises,* which became one of the foundation documents for his new religious community, the Society of Jesus or the Jesuits.

- Dorothy Day—She was an American who lived a rather *laissez faire* life and ended up converting and becoming the founder of the Catholic Worker Movement.

- Thomas Merton—He was an intellectual, poet and *bon vivant* who became a Trappist monk and a great spiritual writer.

❖ Mother Teresa of Calcutta—She was teaching rich girls in Calcutta, India, and decided that her sense of calling was to found a new religious community to serve the poor, especially those who were dying in the streets of Calcutta.

A sense of calling is not necessarily specifically religious. We have many other examples of people who felt a calling to engage in significant work, often that was either dangerous or not understood by the broader population. These would include Mahatma Gandhi, Martin Luther King, Jr., Marie Curie, Amelia Earhart, Cesar Chavez, Rosa Parks, Helen Keller, William Wilberforce, and Nelson Mandela.

In Christian terms, it is our baptism in the Trinitarian formula that is the beginning of our call as a Christian disciple. Then in our confirmation, we are empowered to be adult Christians in the world. Later on, we make decisions about our state of life as a single person, someone who will marry, as a vowed person in religious life, or as a priest. In each of these cases, we are called to take our general baptismal promises and make them applicable in the context of our adult responsibilities. When it comes to specialized vocations, we can trace the trajectory in the following way: a call from God ⟶ a process of discernment ⟶ proper preparation ⟶ approval by the Church ⟶ public validation ⟶ and efforts later on at renewal.

In the end, every Christian has a vocation. As we grow into adulthood, we are entrusted with the responsibility to make good decisions about the form and shape of our lives. For many, this will mean they will marry and raise children of their own. Others will feel a prophetic call to make a difference relative to some great issue of the day. And still others will be called in a specific way to embrace the vowed life and/or serve in one of the ordained ministries of the Church. Whatever our calling, or sense of vocation, the important thing is that we be faithful to it, continue to pray for the guidance of the Holy Spirit, and humbly recognize that, in the end, it is a gift from God.

Conscience

Our conscience is our human ability to discern the difference between right and wrong and, hopefully, to act accordingly. From infancy into adulthood, we go through a process of forming our conscience. That entails recognizing the values that we would like to live by (including those from our religious heritage) and applying them to the decisions of everyday life. In following our conscience, we have an infallible norm for morality. However, we also have a responsibility to form our conscience in light of the existing order of creation. Conscience formation begins in our earliest days and is usually one of the parental responsibilities. Once we go to school, a similar process goes on in the influence that our teachers and other adults have upon us and the ways that we learn to interact with our peers.

It is one of the characteristics of our humanity that we have a moral sense. This refers to a power or faculty that lays at the basis of morality. Sometimes people speak of conscience as a "voice," although it is better understood as a process.

In the formation of our conscience, we are always part of a social process. We need to recognize how much our values and choices are influenced by others, not only those that we respect, but also by the media and peer culture. Our conscience needs to be creative in the sense that we face ever-new challenges to our moral imagination. Just think of the influence of modern medical technology or the various forms of electronic communication or the increased firepower of military weapons or the present means of transportation. We also need to recognize that we will sometimes face moral blockages or gray areas. Life is sometimes ambiguous and we do not always have a ready answer for our moral dilemmas. Our consciences need to be responsible, that is, we need to be prepared to live with the consequences of our choices. If we make moral mistakes, eventually we need to acknowledge them and seek forgiveness. We must also, insofar as it is possible, respect the consciences of others.

In theological discourse, we sometimes differentiate between conscience as a power or faculty and conscience as the exercise of that power. We apply our values to concrete situations and we can sometimes err. We do not always have available to us a full knowledge of the situation or perhaps of the various alternatives. Our consciences can look both backwards to assess how we've done, and look forward to try to make appropriate moral decisions. When our consciences are correct, they are in accord with objective reality. When they are in error, it could be that we just did not know enough and hence are blameless. Or, it could be that we deliberately tried to prevent a full recognition of the circumstances we faced and then we are responsible for our misdeeds.

There are people who suffer from troubling situations of conscience. For example, people who suffer from scrupulosity have a misplaced sense of guilt. They are perplexed by minor issues and have a difficult time ever obtaining a sense of guiltlessness. Others suffer from a perplexed conscience that can never quite resolve what the proper choice would be among various alternatives. And then there are those who suffer from a lax conscience who are basically desensitized morally.

Parents and educators at all levels have a responsibility to help the next generation to be prepared to assume responsibility for their attitudes and behaviors. Sometimes this can take a theoretical turn and involve discussions about different approaches to morality. On other occasions, it can utilize individuals who have led exemplary and heroic lives as ways of inspiring younger people to try to imitate their example. This is why, in Christian terms, we study the lives of the saints and, in secular terms, highlight individuals of great heroic virtue or courage. Relative to the proper formation of conscience is the recognition that, as moral agents active in the world, we are sometimes tempted to betray our own consciences and live immoral lives. When this is the case, we need to have the humility to recognize our sinfulness and turn to other humans and to God seeking appropriate forgiveness.

Integrity

Integrity is defined as firm adherence to a code of moral or artistic values and is connected to incorruptibility. It also suggests a sense of completeness and a commitment to honesty. It might be said that integrity is something we strive for rather than master. It is an effort to chart a path in life that is consistent with our public proclamations. It means, for example, that parents and teachers, who spend some of their time advocating for certain values and ways of life, need to attempt to live by these values as much of the time as possible. That is, in the face of our personal recognition we remain incomplete as sinners and constantly in need of forgiveness and making a new start.

There are a number of obstacles to integrity. The first revolves around our propensity for mixed motives. Even the best things we attempt can have an underlying rationale that we hope never comes to the surface. We can want to be involved in charitable deeds to our neighbor but we may also want to be recognized as an exemplary citizen. In Matthew's Gospel, Jesus warns us that when we pray, or fast, or give alms, we should do so in such a way that we not try to draw public attention to ourselves. On the other hand, there is nothing wrong, per se, with having multiple motives for the same action. That may simply be the way we are made as human persons. The important thing is to try to keep our highest values primary and our other motivations secondary.

One of the chief obstacles to integrity is our capacity for hypocrisy and false pretenses. We must strive to do the right thing for the right reason. Unfortunately, some people spend most of their lives trying to gain attention and end up becoming a prisoner of their hard-won reputations. This can mean that their friends and acquaintances may never be sure about what makes them tick. It is, of course, one of the most significant accusations that a child can make against a parent or a student against a teacher that they preach one thing and act differently.

All of these challenges may simply remind us of our human finiteness. We can strive to have completeness and to be consistent between our values and our activities and forms of conduct, but there is never any guarantee. Even the best of us may succumb, at one time or another, to false motives, hypocrisy, or pretending to be different than we actually are.

We can find good models of integrity by learning more about the lives of the saints. The holy men and women who have gone before us in the life of faith. In particular, the martyrs have been put to the ultimate test and have been faithful until the end. The lives of the saints remind us that many of them struggled day-by-day to be more attuned to what God was calling them to and to be more consistent in their living out of the life of virtue. It was not that they did not experience temptations of a different sort, but, in their final hours, they had the courage of their convictions.

Perhaps the best way to look at integrity is to see it as an aspiration for all of us who have moved into adulthood and have recognized our own human limitations but still aspire to live by our values day-by-day. This can mean resisting peer pressure or taking the initiative in responding to the needs of others or trying to play a leadership role so that we can bring out the best in others. Whatever path our life might take, we can be comforted when our companions on the journey include those whom we can count on and who support our efforts to live faithful to our baptismal and other commitments.

Grace

There is no greater inducement to personal humility than the recognition that all we have by way of talent and resources, including our very existence in the world, comes to us as an unmerited gift. Preceding everything that is, we recognize the creative act of God.

In this light, the birth of Jesus is seen as a pivotal moment in human history when the two great burdens of humanity—sin and death—begin to be overcome. In Jesus' life, death, and Resurrection, we recognize, in faith, that we have been graced; that we, as believers, are people of hope and endless promise.

At one level, grace is a recognition of God's role in our life and history. But, it is also allied with Christ's gift of the Holy Spirit at Pentecost. Through the presence of the Holy Spirit in our individual lives, we can affirm various ways in which we can perfect the exercise of the virtues. By tradition, we call these: wisdom, understanding, knowledge, counsel, piety, fortitude, and fear of the Lord (or recognition of God's sovereignty).

This perspective simply affirms that all of the ways that the world would have us take full credit for our intelligence, wealth, fame, power or social status are based on false premises. Rather, we should constantly be thanking God for whatever good fortune we enjoy, namely, our family and friends, our freedoms, our health, our occupations, and our leisure pursuits.

To be recipients of grace is to be aware that it does not all depend on us. In this light, we can wholeheartedly commit ourselves to lives of service and generosity. Even as we go through the aging process and our natural capacities begin to decline, we can remain confident that Christ will bring all things to fulfillment in the eternal banquet that he has prepared for those who love him.

For people of grace, thankfulness (not pride) is the proper

disposition. Thus, when we celebrate the Eucharist together, we rejoice and we give thanks for the gift of God's only begotten Son whose very body and blood we share as food for the journey.

American Catholicism

In its earliest days, what became the United States was settled by the French and the Spanish. While largely unchurched, both groups came from a culturally Catholic background. It was only with the pilgrims in Massachusetts and later settlers on the East Coast that the early colonies became predominately Protestant. There were pockets of Catholics in a few places like Maryland, but they still were a very small minority.

It was not until the middle of the 19th Century that large numbers of Catholics from Western Europe and later Eastern and Southern Europe came to the states either to flee from persecution or seeking new opportunities. Most of the Catholic immigrants settled in the big cities in the East and later in the Mid-west. There was a minimal presence in the South except for railroad workers and a few members of gypsy groups. The Catholic Church in the United States was dominated in the earliest stages by the Irish. In the wake of the potato famine and afterwards, Irish came in quite large numbers. Because the Church tried to respond pastorally to their presence, it quickly became clear that it was the Irish clergy and Irish hierarchy that would have a dominant presence. The Irish clergy brought with them both their strengths and their weaknesses. They had little appreciation for the intellectual life, they feared radicals in all stripes and forms, and they expected the laity to be obedient to the clerical and hierarchical leadership. On the other hand, the Irish spoke English fluently and they tended to possess refined political skills. Many became members of various government agencies like the police and fire departments, and the post office.

The immigrant Church was largely a blue-collar church since the vast majority of its members were workers with basic-level jobs. Most of the bishops were talented in building churches and schools and other fundamental organizations to serve the pastoral needs of the people. On the whole, they tended to be loyal to the Pope and to the Vatican. From the time of Archbishop John Carroll, the first Catholic Bishop in the United States, up until the present, the Catholic Church has tended to be largely patriotic. They were convinced that the Catholic faith and the democratic system were compatible. Catholic life usually revolved around the parishes and the parochial schools. Catholics also established separate hospitals, orphanages and other social service agencies.

Especially in the big cities, the bishops had a very strong role, not only within the Catholic community itself, but also in representing Catholics to the broader society. They were great fundraisers because of the needs for building so many institutions so quickly. As a group, Catholics did not get involved in many of the public-policy debates of the nation. They had little to say about slavery or the various wars or proposals for economic reform. Instead, they focused on providing the fundamental needs of the large numbers of immigrants that came to this country, usually without many resources of their own. By 1900, 12 million immigrants had settled in the United States, first from Western Europe and later from Eastern and Southern Europe.

Periodically, anti-Catholic groups and movements developed. In response, Catholics defended themselves, but they also became inclined to establish Catholic institutions of one kind or another. For example, they were not satisfied with policies and expectations of the public school system, which were seen as hostile to Catholicism, and therefore experienced the imperative to found schools of their own. Mother Elizabeth Seton founded the Sisters of Charity in the early 19th Century and that became the first American religious community. Later Catholic papers were founded along with the St. Vincent De Paul Society and other not-for-profit organizations intended to serve the social needs of the Catholic laity. During the time before the American Civil War there were some outstanding Catholic leaders, including Archbishop John Hughes in New York City; Isaac Hecker, the founder of the Paulist Order; and Orestes Brownson, a Catholic intellectual. But generally, in the period from the founding of the country until the end of the Civil War, Catholics were more preoccupied with making it in this society, establishing their homes and passing on a legacy to their offspring than engaging in some of the great political debates of the day.

PART TWO

LIFE

REFLECTIONS ON VIRTUES IN THE CHRISTIAN LIFE

This section will focus on how Christian faith is lived out in the circumstances of everyday life. As we grow into adulthood, we can learn the art of moral discernment. We can become more aware of our capacity for good or ill. And, we can recommit ourselves to the grace-filled path to holiness.

Virtue/Vice

Because human beings are goal oriented and creatures of habit, they can conduct themselves properly or poorly toward that which they seek. For one, financial security or a life of pleasure may be what drives them. For others, happiness or social bondedness may be their priority. Our habits can well or ill dispose us. We call good habits virtues and ill habits vices. In both cases, repetition more firmly roots us and non-use moves us in a contrary direction.

In Christian theory, a virtue is sometimes seen as a mean between two extremes. For example, generosity is a mean between extravagance and stinginess and friendliness is a mean between obsequiousness and hostility. To say that a virtue is a mean does not mean that it inclines us to be average or mediocre. Rather, a virtue is a settled disposition of doing good. A virtue makes performance of good actions easier and more joyful.

Some scholars are drawn to a distinction between "intellectual virtues" and "moral virtues." The former direct us toward the truth. They include: understanding, wisdom, science, art, and prudence. The moral virtues dispose the appetites toward good actions. These include: prudence, fortitude, temperance and justice. (Another group of virtues is the "theological virtues," which have God as their object and can only be made known by divine revelation. They are: faith, hope, and love).

In the theory of virtues, the central moral question is: "What kind of person shall I be?" The presupposition is that, if I am the right kind of person, I will do the right things. Underlying all of this is the claim that one can be a good person without being a Christian, but one cannot be a good Christian without being a good person.

Sin

As human persons, we recognize that, while our intentions may be toward the good (which the virtues incline us toward), we are also capable of vice or sinfulness.

In the Scriptures, "sin" is seen as "missing the mark," "being in rebellion from God," "deviating from the right path." Later theological reflection has employed various images for sin:

- Breaking off a personal relationship with God
- Disobedience to God's law
- Pride or love of self
- Unbelief or idolatry
- Participation in certain unjust social structures

I have found certain experiential images just as helpful:

- Being driven from within (by the instinct for survival, by the desire for sexual release, by the pursuit of power)
- Being manipulated from without (by peer pressure, the prevailing culture, advertising, propaganda)
- Infidelity in commitments (being a traitor, devious friend, or adulterer)
- Self-deception (rationalization, a great discrepancy between the inner self and one's public persona)

Christians claim that all human beings are sinners and, therefore, stand in need of salvation (thus the theory of original sin). But, Jesus Christ overcame sin through his death and resurrection. Thus, through faith and a life of love (a virtuous life), Christians can partake in Christ's victory over sin.

In the same way that Christian tradition has specified a number of virtues worthy of emulation, so we named what are called the "seven deadly sins." Vice predisposes us to be ruled by these inherent negative qualities.

The Seven Deadly Sins are:

- ❀ *Pride*—We make ourselves the center of our universe. We become vain, conceited, arrogant, egotistical and selfish.
- ❀ *Envy*—We begrudge the good qualities or the successes of others. This leads us to be sneering, vicious, gossipy, and propagators of gossip.
- ❀ *Anger*—We erupt at the slightest provocation. We become wrathful, revengeful, and violent.
- ❀ *Sloth*—We become indifferent to the important things of life. We are torpid, lazy, apathetic, and emotionally unavailable.
- ❀ *Avarice*—We equate financial success with happiness. We become miserly, wasteful, and excessively acquisitive.
- ❀ *Gluttony*—We allow our appetites to control us. We splurge on food, drink, and petty pleasures.
- ❀ *Lust*—We become prisoners of our sexual urges. We objectify the objects of our desires and seek to manipulate their availability and responsiveness.

There are many other forms of sin that we can name in passing: lying (the violation of truth), drunkenness (the deliberate inducement of a state of unconsciousness and thereby diminished responsibility), theft (wrongfully seizing the property of another), prejudice (treating categories of persons unfairly), blasphemy (denying God's sovereignty), enslavement and torture (violating another's freedom or bodily integrity), murder (taking another's life unjustly).

In the end, virtues are habits that lead us to lives of holiness and vices are habits that lead us to lives of sin.

Prudence

Prudence is considered one of the Cardinal virtues. In the dictionary, it is connected to the ability to govern and discipline one's self by the use of reason or simply good judgment. Prudence has to do with the application of values and priorities to concrete situations of judgment. Sometimes it is thought that with sufficient experience of life one can become a good judge. But there are plenty of counter-examples where people beyond a certain age do not necessarily seem to have learned from whatever experiences of life they have had. Prudence is not simply a function of the aging process. It is rather a skill that accrues to personal insight and self-correction.

Prudence sometimes gets a bad rap. It is thought to accrue to individuals who are hesitant to make judgments or to become active in events. It is then thought to be an attribute to old fogies and people who are simply set in their ways.

Indeed, prudence is just the opposite of fear of change or inactivity. A prudent person necessarily avoids the extremes of rash behavior and inactivity. Rather he or she is ready to take on the challenges of life but does so in a thoughtful and well-balanced way. Prudence is often identified with common sense, which many people remind us is not so common. The best understanding of common sense is that we avoid traps and patterns of misbehavior. Prudent individuals do not rush into the fray without forethought. On the other hand, in situations of emergency where action is necessary, they can be engaged with confidence because of the history of good decision-making that is theirs.

Most of the time prudent decision-making requires a process of analysis, fact-finding and consultation. Good leaders, in whatever walk of life, try to surround themselves with individuals who can represent different points of view so that the final decision-maker can have thought about all of the ramifications of a particular action that is chosen. We often think of the dilemma of unintended consequences and this is simply a reminder that rushing into the fray before proper reflection can lead to results the opposite of what one intended. Just think of some of the recent American military endeavors where passion and a desire to get even has embroiled us in conflicts that seem to have no desired end. In the end, prudence is a characteristic of people that we can trust, who bring out the best in us, who are full of wisdom and insight.

Fortitude

Fortitude is generally considered one of the Cardinal virtues. It suggests that a person possess courage in the face of various challenging circumstances. It implies a kind of fundamental strength of character.

One can think of fortitude with regard to heroism by military actors or individuals who persist in creating artistic objects or those who develop and manufacture new products. Some individuals are known to keep at it no matter what the challenges might be.

As a higher quality, however, fortitude is about living by one's highest personal values, no matter how alluring other alternatives might be. One of the most common motifs in storytelling is to see life as a journey. Such journeys have pitfalls of one kind or another and often involve making it across rivers or scaling mountaintops or persisting in desert crossings. The person of fortitude knows what he or she is seeking and sticks to the plan, with whatever variations, in order to achieve the goal. One of the great religious practices in a number of religions is to go on pilgrimage to some sacred spot. The goal is to make it, but also the journey is an opportunity for self-reflection and self-knowledge. To see our life as a journey or a pilgrimage to God is to recognize the high calling under which all of us stand. Christian believers know that their baptism empowers them to spend their lives seeking God through their service of one another so that at the end of the journey they can be welcomed home into eternal bliss.

One of the biggest challenges for all of us is when we face significant illness, often with circumstances beyond our control. This is the time in which people can display fortitude as they do not let themselves be overwhelmed by what they can't control and focus on healing and a restoration of their health.

Another area of endeavor where fortitude can be seen is athletics, where people often spend years and years of preparation as they seek the final reward, whether it is a medal or a cup, or simply other recognition. Of all the Olympic sports where this seems most evident, I would highlight the Marathon and the Decathlon events. In the Marathon, there are plenty of opportunities to give up from cramps or soreness or simply a lack of will and yet the best Marathon runners are those who make it past those temptations to quit in the midst of the race. The same could be said about those who participate in the ten-event Decathlon, which requires an unusual mix of athletic skills. One has to be patient and do one's best in one event after another knowing that it is the accumulative number of points that will determine the winner in the end. I have always had great admiration for athletes who often do not receive much recognition during the course of the year but who, on the occasion of the Olympics, can achieve their degree of fame and recognition.

In the end, fortitude is best seen as a moral virtue. It can be thought of as the mean between on one hand, the too easy capitulation to obstacles and temptations to give up the pursuit of one's goals and, on the other hand, a failure to recognize that sometimes one has to say, "I have done my best and I should not continue the pursuit beyond my human capabilities."

Temperance

The dictionary connects temperance to moderation in action, thought or feeling, or a sense of restraint. In philosophical theory, temperance is one of the Cardinal virtues. It is the way of thinking about the relationship between our human freedom and what is good for us and good for others. We all know that we have, on occasion at least, binged or gone to an extreme when it comes to eating or drinking or other natural pleasures. When we say someone is addicted, we imply that they lack self-control with regard to some action or desired thing.

Unfortunately, temperance is often connected historically to the "Temperance Movement," when in the United States the voters chose to go dry when it came to the availability and use of alcohol. This was the result of strong advocacy by the Temperance Movement. But we do not really have to adjudicate between the wets and the dries in order to appreciate the value of temperance.

In order to be a temperate person we need to be able to strike some healthy balance between our desires and our actions. For example, most people eat three meals a day and they can examine how many calories and other factors that need to be taken into account to have a balanced diet. But then there is snacking or noshing in which people who normally eat with some degree of self-control take on additional calories simply out of instinct or desire. All of this can offset whatever degree of dietary balance that has been achieved in the choices of foods and drink in the three meals a day.

I have been to some of the poorest parts of the world in which I have seen adults and babies with bloated stomachs who were dying of malnutrition. It is just horrible to view such situations when we recall how much food gets thrown away in American society on a daily basis. World hunger is a structural question and can only be addressed properly by taking into account all the variables. One of my friends is Jim Morris, who for a number of years headed the World Food Bank headquartered in Rome. It was their responsibility to redistribute food that had been donated or purchased to the places in the world that had the most difficult needs to address. It is a wonderful organization and they do an amazing amount of good, but there are still many people—way too many people—dying of hunger everyday around the world.

In the opposite extreme, in this country and throughout much of the developed world, we face the problem of chronic obesity. The search for the perfect diet is a fitting reminder of how hard it is for most of us to avoid the extra calories. It is not simply our intake of food and drink that affects obesity, but also how much exercise we get and what kind of genetic predispositions we carry. However, all you have to do is go out to a mall or watch the crowds at an athletic event to appreciate how much bigger all of us have become.

One of the contributions of American society to the world economy is the notion of fast food restaurants. The appeal of such businesses is understandable; however, the food that is made available through such entities, with regular and abundant use, is one of the great contributors to the obesity epidemic. The same thing is true when it comes to soft drinks and other heavy caloric areas of intake in our diet.

Some people's most effective response to the perpetual lure of unhealthy food and drink is to adopt a more ascetical lifestyle. Some choose to eat only one full meal a day or to forego meat, potatoes, rice, bread and other such foods that are part of a normal diet. Others choose to abstain from alcoholic beverages, not because they struggle with addiction, but because they think that the temperate avoidance of alcoholic beverages is good for them and also a model for those who might struggle with alcohol or other addictive substances.

In some extreme situations, certain cause-related individuals have chosen to forego all nourishment, except water, for extended

periods of time in order to protest some particular law, regula-
tion or structure of control. That was true of Mahatma Gandhi in
India and his ascetical lifestyle drew international attention and,
surely, contributed to the eventual independence of India. The
same might be said to be true to a lesser extent with some of the
IRA members who, while imprisoned by the British, also engaged
in hunger strikes that led to some of their deaths. At a minimum,
this kept the issue of Irish independence in the public eye. One
could say that they engaged in intemperate practices for reasons
that were convincing to themselves.

In the end, temperance is about healthy life choices. These
choices can be motivated on religious grounds, as is true of many
Saints of the Church, or simply to maximize our human freedom
and lifespan. Temperance has historically been considered a virtue
because it is an example of how we are called to find the middle
ground between two extremes. When it comes to food, the two
extremes would be regular overeating and regular undereating. In
both cases, the result can have an extremely negative impact on our
body and on the quality of our very existence in the world.

Classical Notions of Justice

Justice is considered one of the four theological virtues. The
demand for justice is deeply rooted in the human experience of
various forms of violence, despotism, bigotry and unfairness.

The biblical notion of justice in the Old Testament includes fidelity to the demands of the relationship between God, the people,
and the land. When justice prevails, so does peace, prosperity and
fertility. For the Jews, a fundamental test of justice was the concern
for the widow, the orphan, the poor, and refugees in the land.
Underlying all of this was the sense that, in the end, God's justice
would endure despite the sometimes evidence to the contrary.

In the Christian Scriptures Jesus taught that the Kingdom of

God would bring justice into the world. For example, in Matthew's Gospel, Jesus is the teacher of the new righteousness. In Chapter 25 of Matthew's Gospel, in the Parable of the Last Judgment, we have a handy listing of what became known as the Corporal Works of Mercy. All of these are included except burying the dead. In Luke's Gospel there is a strong critique of wealth as an enemy to living a virtuous life. One sign of Jesus' critique of the foolishness of artificial cultural hierarchies was his willingness to share table fellowship with sinners and social outcasts. On the other hand, in Paul's letters, with a pervasive sense that the end was coming soon, there was a tendency to limit the call for social, economic, and political change. Instead, there was a stress on the cross as the source of religious justification.

In both the Jewish and Christian Scriptures, the critique by the Prophets is often directed at those who have taken advantage of others. The classic Jewish prophets called into account wealthy landowners, venal shopkeepers, corrupt political leaders, and others who were enemies of the common good. In Jesus' own preaching, he called for a new sense of community where all were to be considered equal and where love, peace, reconciliation, and justice should prevail.

In the early Church, the tendency was to see problems of justice as revolving around excessive desire for the possession of material goods or the selfish use of them. It was less a problem of possession than one of misuse. Material things were considered good because created by God. However, there was an overarching concern that special attention be directed towards the needs of the poor. Insofar as the Church was a welcoming community, it should be characterized by mutual sharing and support.

Contemporary Notions of Justice

One definition of justice is "To each what is due." In the classical Greek culture, with its strict notion of hierarchy, justice was a function of the role that one played in society. Because slavery existed, slaves had the lowest status and the least claim on the demands of justice. The higher one went in the pecking order of the day, the more that one could appeal to justice to satisfy one's expectations. In the post-Renaissance era, philosophers began to talk about individual rights and possessions. This distinguished the conversation from the earlier emphasis on the coherence of society. Later, Karl Marx made justice focus on basic economic and social needs of the proletariat. Finally, John Rawls spoke eloquently about justice connected to equal liberty and opportunity. These are just two of the individual intellectuals who spoke about justice in one fashion or another.

In the Catholic intellectual tradition, three types of justice have been identified. They are:

- ❧ *Commutative Justice*—This involves an individual's relationship to another individual or one's voluntary group's relationship to another. It demands fidelity to agreements, contracts, and promises. This form of justice tends to be more arithmetical, a kind of *quid-pro-quo.*
- ❧ *Distributive Justice*—This form of justice is concerned with the equal right of all to share in goods and opportunities which are necessary for full participation in the human community. This recognizes that some people are born into privilege and some inherit many obstacles to full participation in society. This could be a function of where they live, their racial, ethnic or religious group, or the impact of economic crises, social disasters or natural events like famines, earthquakes, hurricanes, and tornados. Distributive justice takes for granted that one lives in a sociopolitical order in which laws are fair and properly enforced.
- ❧ *Social Justice*—This form of justice focuses on the responsibility of the State to provide various kinds of organizational structures in the political, economic, and social spheres. Social justice is

entrusted to the various levels of government, including (in the United States context), various cabinet positions that have a responsibility to take care of a cross-section of those entrusted to them. Thus, those who are young or elderly or chronically poor or have some kind of physical or mental limitation or those who are severely ill all have a special claim on our collective attention. That is why discussions about educational policy or ecological concerns across generations or matters of public safety or policies related to agriculture or transportation or communication require high levels of involvement by those with particular expertise.

Each of the three major types of justice has a certain difficulty of realization. But it is inherently easier to try to achieve commutative justice than distributive and social justice. We know from human history that the realization of human justice is always imperfect and partial due to both human sinfulness and to our own finite limitations as human persons.

Another major area of concern with regard to justice revolves around *human rights*. In a liberal democracy or other forms of government that resemble it, we can appeal to certain historical documents like the American Constitution and the United Nations Bill of Rights. These rights are rooted in the freedom of the individual person. They include: freedom of religion, speech and assembly; security of persons and property; *habeas corpus* or the need for evidence in court procedures; and due process of law. In a liberal democracy there is a greater stress on personal freedom and political participation than there is on economic equality and social rights. In an ideal society, we could argue that both are important. But recent political and economic history would suggest that some systems incline toward the first and some toward the second. For example, in Soviet Marxism social and economic rights were preeminent and the Communist party was dominant politically. It also saw history as characterized by conflict across class grounds.

In Roman Catholic rights theory, the whole system is rooted in the dignity of the human person. Among its central affirmations are: the non-instrumental value of the human person; the centrality of freedom; the need for order and unity based on a communion of persons; the special claims by the poor and oppressed; and the necessity and goodness of material conditions, such as health, food, shelter, work, property, and family, that contribute to the well-being of individuals on the margins. Catholic social theory refuses to give exclusive emphasis to either civil and political liberties or to social and economic needs. It proclaims that both are important.

One element of Catholic teaching that is important is called, "The Principle of Subsidiarity." This suggests that the power of government to intervene is real but limited. Matters should be left to the lowest part of the social order in which the desired goal can be achieved. Some things can only be achieved by the federal or state governments. Others can be entrusted into the hands of counties or cities or other municipalities. Others should be left to voluntary associations or civic groups or not-for-profit organizations. In the midst of all of this, the family should be protected as the most fundamental unit of society.

In summarizing Catholic social teaching, David Hollenbach has identified three priority principles. These include:

- ❀ The needs of the poor take priority over the wants of the rich;
- ❀ The freedom of the dominated takes priority over the liberty of the powerful;
- ❀ The participation of marginalized groups take priority over the preservation of an order which excludes them.

There have been various attempts to provide summaries of human rights. One such list includes: matters related to communication, to the needs of the body, to political freedoms, to the freedom of movement, freedom of association, economic opportunity, sexual and familial freedom, and last, but not least, religious freedom.

When any of these is missing, then we have a legitimate area of concern about the extent to which justice has been realized.

Forgiveness

In Chapter 18 of Matthew's Gospel, Peter asks Jesus, "Lord, if my brother sins against me how often must I forgive him? As many as seven times?..." "I say to you not seven times but seventy-seven times." Jesus then goes on to tell a parable about a king who forgives a debtor after he appeals to him and then finds out that the debtor did not forgive someone who owed him as well. The king then goes on to punish the first debtor who did not live by the same standards that he had requested for himself.

The power of forgiveness is one of the great curatives in human life. We have the capacity to say that some harmful thing done against us or some attitude of another person that has undermined our sense of dignity and worth can be overcome by a willingness to say "I forgive you." Of course, this needs to come from the heart and not simply *pro forma*.

When Pope John Paul II went to the prison where the man who had shot him was held, he—in a very public way—forgave him for attempting to take his life. This had a profound impact on many people, including the man forgiven. In a sense, this was an acted parable or a way of making a profound moral point by engaging in a certain kind of activity. In many ways, it is easier to forgive than to forget. Our capacity of memory often means that some event or incident from the past lingers on in our consciousness. Sometimes we have an inability to totally let this go. However, this does not suggest that we cannot learn to forgive the one who has harmed us. This needs to come from our inner resources.

In the teaching of Jesus, the heart of forgiveness is our recognition that it is always reciprocal. As sinners, who in our periods of honesty acknowledge our own misbehavior, we stand in need of forgiveness from the Lord. No one is totally innocent or without fault. Even the best among us need to acknowledge that we have, at least on occasion, failed to live by our own values and standards. That is why we have rituals to acknowledge our sin and seek forgiveness. The most dramatic of these in the Catholic tradition is the sacrament of reconciliation or penance. But even at the beginning of every Mass, we acknowledge our sinfulness and seek forgiveness as well. We pray, "Lord have mercy. Christ have mercy. Lord have mercy." Insofar as we recognize our need of forgiveness from God, reciprocally we should be prepared to exercise in our relationships with one another the same generosity of spirit.

So often in the dynamic of family life, husbands and wives and parents and children have a difficult time letting their grievances go. Those who serve as marriage counselors can give instance after instance where learning how to forgive was at the heart of saving a marriage that had gone on the rocks. What applies to marriage and parenting also applies to other forms of human identification. We can think historically of the so-called feud between the Hatfields and the McCoys. Blood feuds have existed in some societies as far back as we know. We can also think of the dueling tradition that included famous people like Alexander Hamilton and Aaron Burr.

In my lifetime, I have seen the relationship between the United States and its WWII enemies take a 180-degree turn. This is true of Japan and Germany and Italy. We can also think of the warming of relationships between the United States and Viet Nam. These are reminders that if the right people are involved in trying to break down barriers and reestablish cordial relationships, former enemies can in fact become allies, particularly in the economic order. In some parts of the world, tribal, ethnic, and religious struggles are at the heart of various types of conflict. The same is true of religious conflicts that go back centuries. In the final analysis, forgiveness is a profound human willingness to let the past go and to try to forge a more satisfying and hope-filled future. It is never easy to exercise but, after the fact, it can make all of us recognize that, by being willing to forgive an individual and/or group with whom we are at odds, we can also be the recipient of the same generous spirit in return. There is no better formula for trying to promote peace, harmony and reconciliation.

Friendship

A friend is someone attached to another by affection or esteem. It is someone we consider a favored companion. Friendship is a relationship that can only develop across time and depends upon the capacity of both parties. One of the joys of childhood friendships is that they seem to be so serendipitous. They come out of the blue and suddenly one has an ability to share one's life with another in a trusted way.

The friendships of youth eventually develop into the friendships of the teenage years and young adulthood. Often when two people are able to share some of their lives with each other, including some of their most intimate thoughts and feelings, it establishes a bond that, at least for the moment, seems irrevocable. Some friendships develop in the school setting, either because of common academic interests or because of participation in one form of extracurricular activity. Some teammates on a sporting team consider themselves close. The same thing would be true of members of a cast in a theatre company or members of the marching band or those who participate in student government. Most people at that age can tell you the difference between simple companionship and friendship. Some people we just don't find ourselves attracted to or they have some off-putting habits or we don't share enough in common. After puberty, friendships between heterosexual males and females are sometimes precarious. On one hand, they can be among the most satisfying of human dynamics. On the other, the sexuality part of the friendship can get in the way. When people in this society start to date, it is taken as a sign that indeed they share a friendship together. Where this will lead, no one knows, but a dating relationship is more than simply spending time in each other's company.

The friendships of youth, all things being equal, help to develop the capacity for the later adult relationships. Some friendships may simply be the result of having spent a significant amount of time in each other's company. Others may be a function of the allure that one person can have for another and vice-versa. The best relationships seem to be those in which one can comfortably share one's inner self. These relationships are tested across time by the degree of confidentiality and mutual respect that grows out of the relationship.

In the residential college setting, it is often said that this is the moment in one's life when lifelong friendships can begin to be developed. I know that has been true for me. Adult friendship is a result of having achieved a certain level of personal and emotional maturity. It is also a function of having had a wider experience of life, including the experience of the existence of people who are unreliable and sometimes have hostile motives. To know that one lives in a world where some people have evil intentions is to recognize to a greater extent why trusted friends are so important. Friends may appreciate each other more when they are separate physically. Even with all of the forms of modern electronic communication, there is something traumatic about being physically separate from someone that you deeply appreciate and even love.

Some people seem to have a capacity for sustaining a large number of friends simultaneously. This may be a function of their personality or energy level. Others seem to be focused on one or more friendships that have a special quality to them. Whatever the case, a life without friends is a lonely life indeed. That is why being a hermit, or a loner, or a nomad seems to be particularly troubling when it comes to one's emotional stability. Human beings are inevitably social animals and among the relationships that help us to thrive are a certain number of friendships. When one's life is rich with friendships, it seems, for most people, that a particular relationship will move to the next level of personal, cultural, and legal significance. The decision to marry should ideally be based upon the preexisting friendship between the parties that both of them hope will grow over the course of time. The best relationships allow for the other party to change and to grow and to become in some ways a different person than the one they originally interacted with. And this, of course, is reciprocally true. Friendships suffer if they become static or too predictable. There needs to be a certain element of surprise and change to keep the dynamic healthy.

In Christian terms, friendship is one of the forms of love to which we are all called. In Christ we have had it revealed that God is always our friend and we simply need to discover how to most appropriately enter into that relationship. One way of thinking about the Church is that it should strive to become a group of those who gather in Christ's name and strive to become friends with each other. Out of that relationship and mutual trust will grow the capacity to serve society as Jesus has called us to do. One way of thinking about heaven or eternal life is to see it as the great banquet at the end of time when we will be reunited with our friends from this world and have a chance to make an infinite number of new friends that will continue on forever.

Civility

It is common for one generation to lament the practices and mores of the succeeding generation. This often revolves around observations about dress, music, dance, the use of language, and acceptable forms of social interaction. With the worldwide spread of popular entertainment, including television, film, and theatre, as well as various forms of internet-provided material, it is difficult not to be bombarded with the persistent ways in which contemporary culture impacts everyone of whatever age. The elder generation often worries in particular about the impact all of this will have on the youngest members of society.

While I don't generally share this critique, since it has always been somewhat this way across generations, I do think there is a need for a kind word for civility.

In my eyes, civility has to do with manifestations of respect. This would include special privileges for the elderly, the young, and the vulnerable. Simple gestures like holding the door for someone else or helping people to get across a crowded highway, or saying thank you after a favor rendered or sending expressions of appreciation by letter, card, or e-mail are all ways in which these forms of behavior can be reinforced. The opposite of "road rage" is driver civility. This means that we facilitate somebody turning onto a crowded highway from a cross street or a parking lot. It means that on a crowded plane we help put somebody's bag in the overhead bin when they struggle to do so themselves. It means in the loading of passengers that priority is given to those who have some physical limitations or are the parents of children under two.

Civility is one way of recognizing our interdependence as members of a community. It is one way in which we manifest publically that all of us have been the beneficiaries of other people's acts of kindness and it is appropriate for us to reciprocate. In most religious traditions, one of the prime acts of charity is welcoming the stranger in need. In the ancient Middle East, this included not only providing housing and a meal but also washing people's feet or allowing them to cleanse their bodies after a long journey.

Civility also includes refraining from using swear words or offensive language in public places. When the opposite happens, it often shatters the sense of connectedness that people experience. What might seem acceptable in a particular sub-culture, particularly those that are all male or made up of teenagers and young adults, can be seen as offensive in other configurations of people. The exaggeration of bodily noises and other simple human manifestations can also be seen as offensive.

Civility can also revolve around respect for symbols like the American flag, or a menorah, or a crucifix, or an icon, or some other religious object. We do not have to be adherent of a particular religion to know that we have an obligation to respect the things that other people hold sacred.

When I think about examples of civility and kindness, I would list loaning an umbrella to someone when it is raining, providing a ride for someone who will otherwise have to go long distances on foot, sharing a sweater or outer garment with someone who came unprepared for cold weather, giving up a seat on the subway or in a public setting for someone who is elderly or physically limited when there are none available and one is healthier, thanking people who operate behind the scenes of some activity like maids and janitors, waiters and waitresses, chefs and cooks, and those who provide for the common good like police officers, fire fighters, and emergency medical technicians. The gestures may be simple, but they can have a profound meaning.

My hope is that we can preserve and enhance, in American

culture, civility in all of its forms. I am confident that we will be a more integral and responsive civic community if we do so.

Ethics in the Workplace

Christian believers are called to make their way in the world. Except for hermits, members of monastic communities and a few idiosyncratic loners, everyone else needs to recognize that there is no world apart from that which we experience in everyday life. For most people, that means that they will need to work to make a living or derive their financial resources from one or more members of the family who work. In this world of work and civic interaction, Christians are called to be sacraments of God's presence in the world. While this may seem a highfalutin theological concept, it is simply a corrective to those who think that Christians are called to be a kind of sectarian alternative. With this premise in mind—that we have a particular God-given calling in the world that needs to manifest itself in the workplace—I will now discuss several recurring problems that people face in that money-earning capacity.

The first issue is to maintain a concern for truthfulness. In the way that we work, interact with fellow workers, deal with customers, and present a service or product that we are responsible for delivering, it is easy to slide into a kind a gray area. If the role of advertising in whatever format is to present what the company offers in the best possible light, that does not mean that those who are working on behalf of the same company need to buy into the exaggerated rhetoric. If we are honest and straightforward, we usually have a better reception anyway. If the product or service that we are offering is deficient in fundamental ways, we have a responsibility not to deny the obvious. That might entail moving on to a new job or simply holding the leadership accountable for the misinformation that they are providing.

The second issue in the workplace is how to provide fair treatment for all those who work there. This includes hiring processes, evaluation protocols, rewards for good performance, and opportunity for exercising leadership. All of us know that women, members of minority groups, those from outside of our country, and others who have distinguishing characteristics need to be protected in a special way from discrimination, bias, and unfair treatment.

The third issue has to do with fostering personal integrity. This means that, in the various training programs and ongoing education, a high priority should be given to talking about the values of the company, how decision-making best takes place, the opportunities for every employee to contribute to the process, and how both individuals and the corporate whole should be held accountable. It is often when there is a downturn in the economy, some crisis in the organization, or unexpected competition that all of these values are put to the test. It should not depend on hostile lawsuits for companies to abide by their highest values. If it is necessary for people to be laid off, this should be done in the fairest way possible with a full explanation of the circumstances and the prospects for the future. If it is announced that laid-off employees will be rehired if better economic circumstances obtain, then the follow through will be one of the ultimate tests for the company.

It is also the case that companies have external responsibilities to the communities in which they exist. This is why employees should be encouraged to work voluntarily with not-for-profit organizations, or to rally behind a particular effort after a natural disaster, or to be present to one another in times of sickness and death. The way that certain companies that lost many lives on 9/11/01 handled the aftermath for their employees is a wonderful example that should be made available across the board so that it can be followed if similar circumstances exist in the future.

Ethics in the workplace should not be a matter of window dressing or false pretenses. It should be a way of thinking about the role that leadership plays, the kind of values that are passed on to existing and new employees, and the way that the corporate entity sees itself. Over time, this will become one of the most attractive elements for the recruitment of new employees and for the relative reputation of the company in the broader circles of the national and world economy.

The Beatitudes

Matthew's Sermon on the Mount (5-7:27) has a parallel discourse in Luke's Sermon on the Plain (6:20-49). This gives us a clue that the material in each, which may have been uttered on various occasions, represents persistent themes in Jesus' preaching. Matthew's intended readers were Jewish and Luke's were Gentiles (or non-Jews).

In both Matthew and Luke, we have versions of what have become called "Beatitudes" or "blessings." Matthew's version is better known and has been more influential in religious discourse through the centuries. So I will concentrate on the Beatitudes in Matthew.

(1) Import

The Beatitudes are the keynote of the Sermon on the Mount. They announce God's blessings on those who possess and manifest certain dispositions long before the more rigorous demands of the rest of the Sermon on the Mount are laid out. We can claim that the beneficiaries of the rewards promised are people of character. They have made certain moral values their own. Little is said about their life-circumstances otherwise—their age, gender, national origins, or way of making a living. In this sense, the Beatitudes are a kind of universal moral teaching.

The Beatitudes stood (and stand) in contrast with the conventional values that prevailed in the time of Jesus (and today).

Their emphasis on meekness, mercy, peacemaking and purity of heart suggests a kind of counter-cultural existence in the world. There is nothing here about self-assertion; the endless pursuit of wealth, power, and pleasure; public acclaim or the narrowing of one's social circle.

(2) Application

To read through the Beatitudes one by one and to ponder their significance is to be easily overwhelmed by the challenge they offer to our ordinary existence. Who can claim that they are perfect practitioners of all eight proclamations? In my judgment, it is more helpful to identify at least one of the Beatitudes as a lodestone or point of aspiration in one's moral life. Dependent on all the variables of one's concrete existence in the world then we might hope, under the guidance of the Holy Spirit, to become a person who comes closer to realizing one of these ways of becoming a true follower of Christ:

(I) *"How happy are the poor in spirit; theirs is the kingdom of heaven."*

In Luke's version, he contrasts sharply the real condition before God of the poor and the rich. The first is blessed, the other is subject to woe. Matthew is less harsh and more spiritual. Both rich and poor need a spirit of detachment from one's wealth, either as something already possessed or as a preoccupation. The great danger of riches (of whatever kind) is that they will make us feel self-sufficient with no need for God.

In a post-capitalist world, the Beatitudes orient us but do not give us any instructions about how to provide for ourselves and our families, how to interpret our responsibility for the well-being of others, or how to build up the infrastructure of business, education, health care or government. Implicitly, we need a discerning spirit to be poor in spirit in a world full of self-indulgence.

(II) *"How happy the gentle; they shall have the earth for their heritage."*

At first sight, it may seem that gentleness is a function of personality and upbringing. Some seem to have the capacity to interact with others calmly and with tender care. Others seem more confrontative and easily upset. Some seem to have a temper and others to take everything in stride.

In a spiritual sense, gentleness is about respect, mutual regard, a willingness to give the other the benefit of the doubt, and a capacity for distancing oneself from overreaction to fault rendered or imagined. It is not equivalent to naïveté or lack of worldly experience. The gentle person is a boon companion and a worthy friend.

(III)   *"Happy those who mourn; they shall be comforted."*
Eventually, if we live long enough, we all have reason to mourn. We can become overwhelmed emotionally by the death of a family member or friend, the onset of serious illness, a failed pregnancy, the reality of poverty, persistent hunger, natural disaster, or the onset of violent conflict. To mourn is to recognize that sometimes, at least, our life is not under control. We are subject to the vagaries of nature and the human condition. We can be disappointed in ourselves and others.

To mourn is to express our sense of longing, our desire for the restoration of people and circumstances now past. We mourn because we care, because our lives have been disrupted. But mourning is also a time where we can recognize our ultimate dependence on God who can bring all things to completion.

(IV)   *"Blessed are those who hunger and thirst for what is right; they shall be satisfied."*
In Luke's version, the emphasis is on concrete, physical hunger. Matthew takes a more spiritual turn. To hunger for what is right is to focus on the demands of justice in a world full of inequality, prejudice, bigotry, and mal-distribution of the world's goods. It suggests an awareness, not only of our dependencies but also those built into the general social structure. Many go hungry at night, while others struggle with obesity. Some are treated fairly in the hunt for jobs and fitting remuneration and others are not. Some are falsely imprisoned or subject to endless bureaucratic delay or provided an inadequate education and some are not.

To seek what is right is to eventually align oneself with others in the effort to pursue the common good. The bigger and more complicated the issue, the more we need allies and colleagues of a similar mind. The seeking of justice requires passion and persistence and discernment without any guarantees.

(V) *"Happy the merciful; they shall have mercy shown them."*
The achievement of mature self-awareness includes the recognition of one's own failure and sinfulness. No one is immune. Unfortunately, we all have a dark side full of deep regrets. That is why the two great human dilemmas are sin and death. Can I ever be forgiven for my failure and is this life all there is?

Those who practice mercy inherently recognize that it is always a reciprocal demand. We forgive because we stand in need of forgiveness ourselves. The life and ministry of Jesus with his emphasis on mercy, forgiveness, and reconciliation is the backdrop for this comforting blessing.

Sometimes we are called to judge the deed of the malefactor in the normal processes of society. We recognize with horror what human agents are capable of. Yet, the inner world of the offender often remains a mystery to us. Ultimately, we forgive even if it is not appropriate to forget.

(VI) *"Happy the pure in heart; they shall see God."*
Every once in a while, we meet someone who seems so genuine and spiritual and at peace with God that we are inspired by their presence and their example. To us, they seem pure in heart. They are, indeed, the saints in our midst. Some think they are too good to be true. But, if we hear their stories, we come to recognize that they have the same struggles that we do. They have not run away from their humanity but rather have integrated it into their higher calling to be a disciple of the Lord.

In our journey to God, we can be nurtured and encouraged and prodded by the pure of heart in our midst. Their calling is to be antidotes to spiritual lethargy or cynicism. In their company, we can all be full of hope and gratitude.

(VII) *"Happy the peacemaker; they shall be children of God."*
As modern society has grown in scale and complexity, our capacity to kill other humans has been enhanced exponentially. The proliferation of weapons worldwide, the availability of bacteriological, chemical, and nuclear weapons, and the precedent of death and destruction in a succession of modern wars have all made the task of peacemaking all the more challenging.

The peacemaker seeks common ground. He or she tries to recast the grounds upon which violent conflict seems inevitable. Whether at the level of family rivalry or disagreements among friends or neighborhood squabbles or the more potentially lethal involvement in large-scale rioting, terrorist activity, or war, the peacemaker needs to be astute, patient, deeply committed and skillful in seeking solutions that preclude violence.

The best peacemakers historically seem to be those whose personal presence and lifestyle are compatible with the public role of advocacy that they want to play. Sometimes, sad experiences of the past underlay a newfound capacity for successful intervention in the process of peacemaking. Francis of Assisi, Nelson Mandela, and Dorothy Day knew how challenging was the role they felt called to play.

(VIII) *"Happy those who are persecuted in the cause of right; theirs is the kingdom of heaven."*

To be persecuted is to be treated as unworthy of respect, as a plaything of history. Often, the persecution is a function of the accident of one's birth, religious faith, or political position. Sometimes, persecution is a function of the personal role one has played or what one is thought to represent. But, just as easily, it may result from groupings that one is identified with by hostile forces in the political order. Tyrants see enemies everywhere.

For Christians, persecution is often connected with matters of faith and belief, fundamental bedrocks of one's baptized commitments. That is why the early Church often celebrated Mass on top of the bones of the martyrs. Some Christian martyrs welcomed their persecution and death as an opportunity to testify to their faith in Christ and the promise of the Resurrection.

Today, more Christians suffer persecution worldwide than any other group. We honor them and pray for their release, we also seek to be inspired by their wholeheartedness and sterling example.

Concluding Remarks

Mahatma Gandhi once said that he had read the Sermon on the Mount (including the Beatitudes) with great admiration and appreciation for the profundity of the teaching. His problem was that most of the Christians he met did not seem to be living by its dictates.

Our challenge, in light of Gandhi's criticism, is to take the Beatitudes seriously. If we can but find one Beatitude as our guiding light, maybe our incompleteness as Christian disciples can be overcome.

The Virtues of a Religious Community

In the Christian life, both the individual and the group have a need for spiritual development. When new members join a religious community, they need to be initiated into the practices of the group as well as its traditions. One of the ways that religious life gets reformed occurs when individuals test out their vocation within the group and the religious community makes decisions about those who have a proper call to become members under vows. Both the individual and the group need the gift of judgment or discernment.

There are five virtuous qualities of the common life that should characterize the common life of a religious congregation and that should attract new members who have a legitimate vocation. They are:

(I) *Consistent Prayerfulness*—There are a wide variety of structures of prayer in religious life from the rigors of contemplative life and monasticism to the less-demanding style of apostolic-oriented communities. In the Congregation of Holy Cross, we commit to daily Mass, the recitation of the Office, and other forms of piety according to personal preference. When possible, we pray these in common but not to the detriment of our primary apostolic commitments. The important thing is that we seek to place Jesus Christ at the center of our lives.

(II) *Spontaneous Generosity*—This mode of living together should flow from the love and mutual respect by all participating in the common life. Out of an overflow of genuine concern, a spirit of service and a willingness to get engaged in the needs of others can be the undergirding of a high quality of personal bonding.

(III) *Affectionate Support*—This usually begins with time shared together and the friendship that results, starting with one's peers, but, over time, extending across the various age groups and apostolic situations. Such support recognizes the uniqueness of each person. Every member may not be equally likable, but one learns a spirit of tolerance and a willingness to give and take. The practice of saying thank you or writing notes of congratulations can be a fitting recognition of the role that people play in the life of the community.

(IV) *Diligent Labor*—In community life, one is called to use one's talents in the service of others. First of all, we are called to persistence in the task at hand, which is often the assigned obedience that one participates in. It may also include a willingness to serve in roles of leadership or administration. Such willingness to work hard toward a common goal gives confidence to everyone that we are all in it together and can count on each other in a pinch.

(V) *Leisurely Presence*—Not only is community life about prayer and apostolic engagement but it also requires being available to each other on a daily, weekly, and yearly basis. The common life needs to be constantly nurtured through the initiative of individuals and the willingness of everyone to participate. The healthiest religious communities know how to have fun together whether it is going out for a meal or attending a play, movie, or athletic event together. Annual retreats and the celebration of anniversaries can be other festive moments.

At its best, a religious community resembles high-quality family life. It unites its members across generations and across the circumstances of shared ministry. New members are welcome with openness and enthusiasm and old members who move into retirement or undergo sickness can experience the vibrant support of others. When a member dies, the rituals of eulogy, funeral Mass and burial can be an important moment in which all can celebrate the life of the deceased member, while, at the same time, reaffirming their presence and mutual support of each other through all the stages of life.

Passing on the Faith

Faith as a Heritage

For most of us, especially those who have been baptized as children, our faith is passed on to us by our parents and family members. This includes participation and worship, the use of religious language, and examples of people who live a life with meaning and integrity.

Faith is also passed on to us in our peer group, especially in Catholic schools, by both our teachers and those with whom we affiliate. Faith can also be what we learned in a more intellectual way by memorization and reflection about central teachings of the Christian community.

Faith needs to be learned according to the stages of life. In elementary school, it is appropriate that it be simple, include the authority of teachers and significant adults, and appeal to our sense of wonder and mystery. In high school, we are better prepared to deal with complexity and the need for socialization and the desire for independence. Little by little, we are in the process of making the faith passed on to us part of ourselves. In college, depending on what kind of school we attend, we may be in the company of unbelievers or those who are skeptical about religion. We have to deal with both personal doubt and cultural hostility. It is always helpful if we are in the company of those who have integrated their faith convictions with their style of life. As young adults, we need to test the integrity of our teachers, our parents, and public officials. In the end, it is desirable that our faith commitments be our own.

Though faith as a heritage and faith according to the stages of life are important considerations, we also need to deal with our exposure to the alternatives to faith. These include indifference, experimentation, and the desire for pleasure. Indifference can spring from our preoccupation with activity and a here-and-now orientation. It can also be a function of the lack of a sense of personal presence or involvement in problems of one kind or another that revolve around health, self-confidence, and parental support. Experimentation is natural as part of the growing process into adulthood. We can look for the thrill of discovery and the lure of the unknown. Sometimes this leads adolescents into paths that are personally destructive. On the other hand, it may simply be part of being exposed to a complex world. In adolescence we also have a desire for pleasure and this can revolve around the cult of the body, seen for example in the preeminence of athletics or bragging about sexual prowess or being preoccupied with one's personal appearance. It can also involve the cult of the mind where people begin to think of themselves as smarter or more astute than their peer group or the broader society. There can also be a kind of escapism that revolves around pleasure where people cultivate their own sense of clothing, lingo, music, and esoteric rituals. Finally, when an adolescent has the experience of genuine faith, it is important that it be highly personal and not simply a function of parental pressure. It needs to be genuine—that is voluntary and intentional. And it must be vital—that is, enthusiastic and energetic. For many adolescence in high school and college, the experience of faith exploration in peer groups is both desirable and reinforcing. The more that one's personal faith in adolescence is reinforced by one's parents, family, friends, and peers, the more likely it is that it will be sustained through the next stages of life.

REFLECTIONS ON WAR AND PEACE

Among the major moral issues of our day, none is more perplexing than how to think about the relationship between Jesus' teaching in the Gospel about peace, reconciliation, and forgiveness and the huge loss of life that we have seen perpetrated across the centuries, by human beings, including that inflicted by Christian believers. In this section, I will appraise the three major approaches to violence on behalf of the state that Christian theologians have developed as well as certain correlative issues.

Christian Pacifism

Scriptural Background

The Sermon on the Mount, the fifth chapter of Matthew's Gospel, is at the heart of Jesus' teaching about war and peace. We hear refrains like "Happy the peacemakers, they will be children of God." We hear that we are called to be peacemakers and agents of reconciliation. In the so-called Sixth Antithesis on the Law, we hear the connection between anger and violence and we are encouraged to turn the other cheek. It is said that the *lex talionis*, or law of retaliation, has been replaced by the way of peace. We are encouraged to love our enemies and pray for our persecutors.

Not only did Jesus teach the way of peace, but he also manifested it in the Garden of Gethsemane when he chided Peter for drawing his sword to defend him. He said, "Those who use the sword will perish by it." We can also look back at Luke's depiction, in chapter three, of Jesus' temptation in the desert. He acknowledges that he could use angelic armies to force people to follow him, but this is not the route of messiahship.

Jesus is pictured over and over again as the Prince of Peace, not as a warrior God or someone seeking to control the world or create disciples by violence. Stephen, the first Christian martyr, imitates Jesus' own death, as do so many of the subsequent martyrs. To become a martyr—that is, to give one's life for spiritual integrity—is indeed following the example of Jesus.

In addition to Jesus' teaching and example, there were other reasons why the Christians in the first generation were not members of the Roman military. The Romans, reflecting their willingness to vary their legal expectations from culture to culture, did not require Jews to become members of the military. They were thought to be unreliable soldiers, thereby would not add anything to the strength of Roman control over the extremes of the empire. Insofar as Christians were thought of as a sect of the Jews, they were not required to become members of the military either. In fact, there was a much greater temptation by Christians to follow the example of the Zealots who resisted the Romans, sometimes to the point of taking up arms. One of the strategies of the Zealots was to use knives to attack military soldiers when they were isolated from their comrades. They were called "Sicarii." One of Jesus' apostles was called Simon the Zealot, which suggests that he may have had some historical participation in the movement.

It is fair to say that, in the first generation of Christians—that is, the immediate disciples of Jesus and those who are depicted in the Acts of the Apostles and in the Pauline epistles—there were no examples of Christians joining the military. To the contrary, Christians would have been described by their contemporaries as a peaceful group in their common life and in their attitude toward military violence.

Christian Pacifism from the Early Church
up until the Contemporary Period

The early Christian community was regularly persecuted by the Roman Empire. They were considered a minority religion and were relatively uninfluential. Most of the early Christian theologians were consistently pacifist in their orientations, even though their theological arguments varied.

Among the reasons that Christians would have rejected service in the army were: the propensity toward emperor worship, including in the taking of an oath to belong to the military; a relatively dissolute lifestyle for the Roman military members; the inability to marry and the prevalence of camp prostitution; and the possibility that they would be called upon to persecute fellow Christians. By the Second Century, however, some Christians were in the Roman army when they were converted. It was easier to tolerate such a mixed status when they primarily served as firefighters, police, mail deliverers and guards. In the preaching of the Christian community, among the titles given to Jesus were Paschal Lamb, Suffering Servant, and Prince of Peace. He was pictured as the friend of the poor and the outcast, not as someone who sought political power and influence. In fact, the cross became the great Christian paradox. Almost all of the Apostles are understood to have been martyred except for St. John. The martyrdoms of Peter and Paul in Rome received much attention and that is why the Churches dedicated to them today have been for centuries places of pilgrimages.

After Constantine in the Fourth Century, in a series of decisions by the Roman Empire, pacifism began to decline and became a minority position. It was continued primarily in monasteries.

The ascendency of the Roman Empire throughout much of Europe and Asia meant that Christianity had a stake in the well-being of the political government as well. It was not until the Middle Ages that there began to be Christian pacifist sects like the Waldenses, the Lollards, and the Brethren. At the time of the Protestant Reformation there were certain sects that were pacifist in their orientation as well, including the Mennonites, the Amish, and the Quakers. More recently in the Catholic world we have seen, in the United States, the development of the Catholic Worker Movement under the leadership of Dorothy Day and Peter Maurin. In addition, we have seen the witness of Gordon Zahn, Thomas Merton, and the Berrigan Brothers.

During the Viet Nam War, there were many more Catholics presenting themselves as conscientious objectors than had been true in WWI, WWII, or the Korean War. Part of this was a function of the draft, but it was also influenced by a rethinking of the acceptability of violence by nation states.

The irony of history is that Christians went from being exclusively a pacifist group in the early days to being primarily a just-war group through much of the history of the Roman Empire, on through the most recent wars. However, in recent years Catholics have looked more critically at the issue of the role of the military in light of the power of modern weaponry, particularly atomic, biological, and chemical weapons.

An Assessment

Pacifism through the centuries has been subjected to multiple critiques. On the pro side is the overwhelming witness of Jesus and the early Church. In many ways, it is the only pure position. It gives a priority to love, mercy and forgiveness, one of the criteria developed in the parable of Matthew 23 about the last judgment. We also have the example of the Good Samaritan. Many would point to the futility of war as seen in the history of humanity. The scale and power of modern weaponry has raised this debate to the next level.

We know from human experience the perpetual temptation to the expansion of war. We see this in not only inter-generational feuds, but also in the long historical memory of ethnic, religious, and national groups. Our memory often focuses on past affronts and prevents us from learning to forgive and forget.

President Dwight Eisenhower, at the end of his term of service, gave a talk about the military industrial complex, which is a reminder that a lot of money can be made by providing armaments, supplies and services to military organizations. The United States is the largest producer of arms and they need buyers. Sometimes we find that some of the poorest countries in the world are big buyers of military goods either to prop up a dictatorial government or simply to have on hand in case there is civil unrest. There is always the problem of new weaponry and how long it becomes state of the art. For every offensive weapon that is created there needs to be a defensive weapon in response. In the United States, in particular, but also in some of the other developed countries, defense budgets grow exponentially, often without any significant debate.

One of the biggest concerns about the role of the military revolves around what can become the idolatrous pretentions of the state. Everything then begins to revolve around patriotism and whether you are for us or against us. Propaganda becomes commonplace and it becomes hard for individual citizens to dissent from what is the ascribed role of the military on behalf of the nation.

The con arguments against pacifism include:

❀ The inadequacy of its theory of human nature—Since most of us do not live in monasteries, but rather live in this world, it seems from our everyday experience that sometimes we need to resist evil in one form or another. We know that chaos is unacceptable; all you have to do is look at the recent histories of places like Rwanda and the Congo, not to speak of Syria and Afghanistan, to realize how many people suffer when there is no organized government that has status and effectiveness. There is always the old question: "What would you do if _____?"(fill in the blank)—for example, "if someone in your family was being attacked or some innocent stranger that you could protect from harm or the most vulnerable part of the population?" Would you not feel an obligation to use violent means if necessary for a greater good? There is also the question about how important the loss of fundamental freedoms is to any of us and all of us collectively. Are we prepared to accept life under Godless totalitarianism?

❀ Pacifism seems to make war into the central moral issue. Why don't we concentrate on other, more important, human values as well like poverty or the rights of minorities or integrity in personal life or whatever it might be?

❀ Pacifism seems to be dependent on a literal interpretation of scripture. Cannot the Sermon on the Mount be seen as an ideal to be striven for rather than a direct prescription? The Old Testament text seemed to be full of violent behavior sometimes described as under the authority of God. Isn't the Bible to be seen as a whole, with the New Testament helping to clarify some of the religious values that have emerged under Israel's status as a chosen people?

❀ There seem to be different types of pacifism, including absolute and relative. Absolute pacifists are opposed to war and violence in any form. Relative pacifists may condemn particular wars or forms of war but are open to the possibility that violence may need to be used in a good cause if the common good can be properly served. Mahatma Gandhi developed his own distinctive view of pacifism that he called *satyagraha*, which means truth force." It was intended as a basic philosophy of life using non-violent resistance as a means toward an end.

I personally am not a pacifist even though I can recognize its appeal. I see it as a way of critiquing our too-ready acceptance of the level of violence we see in the world around us, often used by nation states or other levels of government. Insofar as we can, we need to be instruments of peace, justice, and reconciliation. Unfortunately, sometimes this will lead us to the use of force, even weapons, in defense of the innocent or a good cause. This is an unfortunate side effect of the evil that we see around us and the capacity for evil that all of us possess.

Just War Theory

Historical Considerations

Just War theory has an inherent appeal as an attractive mix of idealism and pragmatism. Insofar as it can, it tries to put into practice the fundamental teachings of the Gospel about peace, forgiveness and reconciliation. But, it also recognizes the existence of evil in the world, the mixed motives that underlay human activity, and the need for protection of national sovereignty and the innocent.

Just War theory is not explicitly Christian. It was inherited from various Greek and Roman thinkers. Underlying it was the desire for the vindication of justice and the restoration of peace. It functions as a kind of Code of War. Aristotle, who was quite influential in the thinking of St. Thomas Aquinas, coined the term "Just War." He was interested in fostering a way for the Greek city-states to oppose various barbarian invaders. Later, Cicero saw it as a code for conquerors. He did not think that the Roman Empire could tolerate rebellion. Often, in his thinking, Just War came down to total war. When fighting the barbarians all means were valid. It was up to the college of priests to determine when wars were valid.

After the Edict of Milan in 313 AD, the Church became connected with the Roman Empire. In about 416 AD, Emperor Theodosius had excluded pagans from the Roman army. As a result, the well-being of the Roman Empire and of the Christian Church were coterminous. St. Ambrose saw Just War as a means of connecting the defense of the empire with the defense of the faith. In his eyes, pacifism was limited to the clerical and private sphere.

The first great theoretician among Christians of Just War was St. Augustine of Hippo. In his classic, *The City of God*, he saw the Roman Empire as the provider of order versus pagan chaos. It should be remembered that late in his life the Roman authority in North Africa, where he resided, was under attack from various forces. Augustine saw that, as a result of sin, the use of violence was tolerable in the earthly city. He also acknowledged the horror of war. Eventually, Augustine articulated some of the major elements of subsequent Just War theory, namely, proper authority, a just cause, last resort, and proper intention. Those who engage in violence morally did so as agents of the state.

In the Middle Ages in predominately Christian Europe there was an effort to limit the scale of extensiveness of war. This took two forms in particular. First, there was the Peace of God, which exempted certain categories of people and certain places from violence. These included women, children, old people, and other non-combatants. Among the places would be churches, monasteries, and other sanctuaries. The second effort to control violence was called the Truce of God, which exempted certain times in the calendar year from violence, namely, Christmas, Easter, Sundays and certain seasons. The hope was that, by having these periods of truce, peace might become expected by those who had some experience of non-violence.

St. Thomas Aquinas lived in a time in which the Holy Roman Empire was breaking apart. He knew of the Crusades and the Inquisition. Many of the small city-states were centered in castles and armed knights engaged in much of the violence. In the face of all of this, Thomas emphasized the importance of proper authority, just cause, and right intention. He saw war as neutral and was primarily interested in the manner in which war was engaged. In the 14th and 15th Centuries in Europe, national consolidation was going on. There was also an increase in the potency of weapons, like the longbow, cannons, and standing armies. By the 16th and 17th Centuries, there was constant war in Europe, on the seas in the time of colonial expansion, and in the Americas. Europe saw constant participation in wars of religion. Both Martin Luther and John Calvin, the two great fathers of Protestantism, were Just War defenders. Luther in particular articulated his Two Kingdoms Theory where what was unacceptable to the individual agent operating independently was possible when one was serving on behalf of the well-being of the state. Luther wrote a famous treatise on whether a Christian could become a soldier and his answer was yes, as long as he was serving as an agent of the state in which he resided.

Finally, closer to our own time and history, International Law developed in response to the horror of more contemporary warfare. The Red Cross was developed as an agent of medical care for those who had been harmed in warfare. There was an expectation that prisoners of war should be treated fairly. There was also a growing sense of consensus about the prohibition of certain weapons, for example, the use of mustard gas after WWI. The same could be said about the use of atomic, bacteriological, and chemical weapons after WWII.

This is a simplified version of how Just War theory developed. In fact, it was quite complicated with many different participants in the debate. Today, in the Catholic Church, the overwhelming consensus is that Just War theory can be seen as an appropriate response to the existence of violence and evil in the world. The problem, however, is how to make sure that the various criteria are enforceable and that people, heads of state and other members of the military, are held accountable for the violations of these standards.

Assessment

As the Just War theory has evolved, there has been a relative consensus about the fundamental criteria that make it up. Generally, these criteria are divided into two sections. The first has to do with the decision to go to war in the first place. Among the criteria in this area are four fundamental standards. They are: just cause, legitimate authority, last resort, and right intention.

Just cause makes reference to the vindication of justice, national self-defense and the hope for restoration of peace. Legitimate authority is usually self-evident, but in circumstances of civil war or high levels of unrest, it may be difficult to discern who the appropriate authority really is. Last resort presumes that negotiations have gone on and that there are no premptive attacks. Right intention has to do with what lies in the minds and hearts of those who make the decision, namely, the seeking of peace with justice, the absence of revenge and a commitment to moral means in the execution of the war.

The second set of standards has to do with the way in which wars are waged once they are undertaken. The central standards here are non-combatant immunity, proportionality, and humane treatment. Non-combatant immunity presumes the capacity for discrimination between direct and intended attacks and the sometimes-regrettable collateral impact on civilian populations. The difference between Just War theory and Total War theory is that the effort is made to preserve this fundamental distinction about who can be targeted. With the scale of capacity of modern weaponry, this is a very difficult criterion to preserve. Think of the wholesale bombings of cities, the use of atomic, bacteriological or chemical weapons or the employment of IED's (improvised explosive devices).

The second standard of proportionality attempts to gauge that a greater good can be achieved by the war than the evil that is suffered. In order to make this decision there needs to be an analysis of the impact on people, property, culture, and the operative moral standards of the society. Humane treatment presumes that no torture will be used, that there will be no use of certain types of weaponry, that the status of prisoners of war will be protected, and that there will be no demand for unconditional surrender. When it comes to the assessment of Just War theory by those who favor or oppose it, a lot of arguments have been assembled on both sides.

On the con side, we recognize that the theory is not explicitly Christian and that it may have been adopted on the grounds of survival or convenience. There was for a period of time, especially in the Roman Empire, the fear that the Church could be destroyed by outside forces. In fact, the historical evidence is rather dreary about whether the Just War theory has ever been effectively implemented. Some would point to WWII as an example of an actual Just War. The formation of the United Nations was an attempt to reach some kind of universal consensus about conflict and who may have violated basic human rights. But the United Nations has no effective power in enforcing even its own standards. Another argument revolves around the number of indiscriminant weapons that prevail like landmines, rockets, the neutron bomb, ABC warfare and the use of gas bombs in WWI. It is hard, even with a relatively small nation-state, to determine who is responsible for the misdeeds in war. Another factor has to do with the power of propaganda and the way in which the enemy side is often pictured in sub-human terms. Somewhat peripheral, but also important in their own terms, are the viability of a draft in gaining members for the military and the use of military chaplains.

The arguments in favor of the theory of Just War revolve around the mix of idealism and practicality. It is seen as a means to protect the innocent and to oppose evildoers. This is best seen in an analysis of the role of the police in democratic societies where just about everyone can agree that those who intend to violate the law in a significant way should be held accountable for their misdeeds and that the law enforcement agencies should do everything they can do to hold the miscreants accountable. Just War theory with its criteria is one viable way to think about the use of violence in human conduct on behalf of the state that avoids the seeming idealism and utopianism of pacifism and the almost absence of criteria of accountability that goes along with the so-called Crusade mentality. If nothing else, Just War criteria and their further amplification can help us think about the difficult moral challenges we face as citizens of a country and a world that includes the existence of those who would do harm to us and our way of life.

The Crusades

The Hebrew Scriptures are full of examples of the shedding of blood either literally or figuratively. For example, we see in Genesis 9:5 that the shedding of blood is appropriate in response to violence. In Psalm 137, we hear that we are encouraged to bash our enemies' babies on rocks, and in Psalm 144 to prepare our hands for war and our fingers for battle. The Jews had a term, *herem*, which describes the Holy Wars of Israel. We see that in the armies of Moses and Joshua, of David and Goliath. The Israelites were encouraged by the notion that Yahweh fought with them. They were prepared to spare no life in enemy towns and to kill all of the male children.

The sense of war that we have in parts of the Jewish Scriptures is that war was at God's command, that ruthless tactics were justified, that there was no demand for non-combatant immunity, and that the priests legitimized the conflict. For example, the Promised Land was occupied and therefore required military engagement in order to win it for Israel.

In a sense, the wars of Israel stand as the backdrop of the Christian Crusades. In 1095, Pope Urban II called the first Crusade, which was purportedly about gaining access to the Holy Land for pilgrims. It was also intended to end internecine warfare among Christians in the nations of Europe. Unfortunately, it also entailed the persecution of Jews in Europe. The first army was made up of peasants and was destroyed. But the second army was able to capture Jerusalem. When they arrived in the Holy City, they slaughtered all of the Jewish and Muslim residents. The second and third Crusades in the 12th Century were failures militarily and at best gained mixed results. The fourth Crusade ended up being fought against the orthodox Christians. Constantinople was pillaged and the Latin empire was created. There was also in the 13th Century a Children's Crusade, which was a total fiasco and a complete aberration. The fifth, sixth, seventh, eighth, and ninth Crusades were at best indecisive, but generally considered to be failures. It became unclear what the goal was and it was more difficult to gain support from the ruling authorities in Europe. By the end of the 13th Century, much of the Holy Land was under the control of the Muslims.

In retrospect, we could say about the Crusades as a movement that they reflected a theocratic notion of government where God was seen to be on our side. They were justified by Popes and often the enemy was seen as demonic. The banner of the Cross was intended to suggest that those who participated had primarily religious motivations, but that was seldom the case. When it came to the means of warfare, the Crusades knew no constraints. All means were seen to be licit. There was also an economic motive since the victors got the spoils. As the Crusade movement unfolded, there was a shifting sense of purpose. The Crusades did establish trade routes between Europe and the Middle East that served the purposes of the royal leadership. By some, it was seen as a means of spreading Christianity in the Muslim world, but this was not in any way successful. Some of those who participated as Crusaders went as a means of atonement for serious sin and a form of penance.

The Crusade mentality is a perpetual Christian temptation. It is a way of picturing the world as divided between the forces of good and the forces of evil, kind of like the *Lord of the Rings*. We can see the same mentality in the way video games are constructed. Crusades are closer to the mentality of Machiavelli than the Christian gospels. Much of the inherent cruelty of the Crusades passed over into the movement in Europe called the Inquisition.

The Inquisition

The Inquisition as an agency began in 1231 as a way to combat heresy, at first directed against the Albigensians. By 1254, the use of torture had been justified by Pope Innocent. The rationale was that it was the best way of determining who was guilty and it was surrounded by various legal protocols. The Inquisition in one form or another went on for centuries.

In the 15th Century in Europe, we see the witch trials in which over 200,000 women were put to death under the suspicion that they were in league with Satan. The same could be seen in the United States in the Salem witch trials.

The Spanish Inquisition began in 1478 as a government agency, separate from Church control. It was directed toward Muslims and Jewish converts who were under suspicion. At the head of the Spanish Inquisition was the Grand Inquisitor and there were no appeals to his judgment. The infamous Torquemada led a reign of terror.

How the Inquisition could possibly be justified on Christian grounds is beyond me. Its goal was to seek the truth but it presumed that the methods of torture and intimidation would be reliable, which they are not. The Inquisition gave religious sanction to a despicable method of trying to seek the truth. The Inquisition was endemically opposed to any kind of change, whether of theological articulation or Church structure. In the New World, it became an instrument of dominion.

We can look back now on both the Crusades and the Inquisition as a terrible failure of Christian moral accountability. Both arose out of theocratic pretentions where the fate of the Church and State were seen as coterminous. It employed the harshest methods possible in order to preserve certain religious prerogatives. The result was a reign of terror that knew no bounds. Surely, many of those involved thought they were doing God's will. From our vantage point in history, they had taken over totalitarian means of maintaining control and given them a Christian underlay.

Let us hope and pray that the mentality reflected in both the Crusades and the Inquisition never returns as a temptation for Christian believers.

Nuclear War

Thank God, there have only been only two uses of atomic weapons against human populations. The first was in Hiroshima, Japan, on August 6, 1945, where 80,000 people were killed instantly and 70,000 more died within a month, 60,000 homes were destroyed or damaged and somewhere around 365,000 people were affected by the explosion. Then on August 9, 1945, in Nagasaki, Japan, 24,000 people were killed instantly and 138,000 were affected. The great irony about Nagasaki is that it was the center of the Christian community in Japan.

For a period of time, the United States had a monopoly on nuclear weapons. But then in 1945 they were joined by the Soviet Union, in 1952 by Britain, and in subsequent years, by France, China, India, Israel, and North Korea.

The effects of nuclear explosions are traumatic and drastic. They include deadly ionizing radiation, shock waves, searing heat, a firestorm, asphyxiation, and nuclear fallout. It basically leads to the destruction of the infrastructure of a society.

Nuclear weapons can be delivered in a wide variety of forms, including from airplanes, ships, submarines, and from land-based missiles. During the Cold War, missiles were placed in silos by both sides and on movable bases so that it would have been impossible to wipe out all of the other side's nuclear weapons at one time. Over time, the missiles became smaller and more mobile. With the proliferation of nuclear devices, various governments attempted to develop various deterrent strategies. These included:

- ❀ "Counter-combatant"—in which there would be no targeting of civilian populations;
- ❀ "Counter-force"—target military first and later civilians;
- ❀ "MAD" Mutual Assured Destruction—This was sometimes referred to as the rationality of irrationality since it deliberately attacked cities with large concentrations of population. Because the result would be so devastating, it was thought to be irrational for the other side to employ their weapons in this fashion. It was said to increase the improbability of the use of nuclear weapons.

Many of us thought that after the fall of the Soviet Union and the SALT talks and the attempt to decrease the number of nuclear weapons around the world that we had moved beyond the need to be concerned about nuclear war. However, we find with rogue nations like North Korea and Iran that there is a growing concern that once again nuclear weapons could be put into use.

In terms of moral analysis, the obliteration bombing of cities like Hamburg, Dresden, and Tokyo in WWII clearly violated the criteria of "Just War." There was a deliberate attempt to destroy industrial cities by incendiary devices and explosives. This was intended to destroy the infrastructure and also to terrorize the local population. This was non-nuclear, but had some of the same impact. Atomic, bacteriological, and chemical warfare all suffer from the same moral defaults—they are unable to be controlled and they have a huge negative impact on large numbers of people. Nuclear war violates two principles of "Just War," that is, the principle of discrimination, which attempts to preserve non-combatant immunity, and the principle of proportionality, which tries to limit the impact of various forms of war on the civilian population.

In 1983, the U.S. Catholic Bishops issued a letter titled "The Challenge of Peace." It was drafted by a committee, went through three drafts, open discussion, and passed on the final vote. It included the following affirmations:

- A presumption against war;
- The national right and duty to self-defense against unjust ag-
- gression;
- No offensive war;
- No indiscriminate destruction of whole cities or population centers;
- The principle of proportionality;

  Deterrence can be accepted as a step on the way toward progressive disarmament. It cannot be intended as immoral strategy. It is not acceptable as a long-range strategy.

As follow-through, the letter recommended support for immediate, bilateral, verifiable agreements. It also recommended deep cuts in nuclear arsenals and a comprehensive test ban treaty in the prevention of nuclear proliferation.

The letter had a number of critics on the conservative side of the political equation in the United States.

In my opinion, with the destructive capacity and number of nuclear weapons available to many parties today, any re-initiation of nuclear war would be a horror for humanity.

PART THREE

NOTRE DAME

REFLECTIONS ON NOTRE DAME

This section draws heavily on my experiences on the Notre Dame campus as a teacher, pastor, preacher, and administrator. While the examples I draw on are particular to Notre Dame, I think they have wider application.

Ten Words of Advice for a Successful First Year of College

1. *Never eat alone*—Especially for those who live in student dormitories in residential campuses, it is important to establish a social basis for one's life. At Notre Dame we have all four years living together in common in one or another dormitory. Whatever dormitory one lives in, there is a regular dining hall opportunity for meals. It is not unusual for residents of the dorm to establish a table or two that are regular hangout spots for fellow members of the dorm. The most exasperating experience for a new student is to go over to the dining hall and feel utterly alone because you cannot recognize any of the faces. It seems like everybody but you has a friendly face or companion that one can be comfortable with. That is why it is important to find the location of the favored tables for members of one's dorm so that one can simply sit down, begin a conversation, and presume that one will be welcome. Once a certain routine is established and one begins to feel somewhat at home, it becomes easier each time that one makes the trip to the dining hall. It is even better to turn to one's roommate or next-door neighbors or other new students living in the dorm so that you can make the trek over to the dining hall together.

   It is not surprising that new students in college could feel anxiety attacks about not fitting in or being rejected or somehow having a difficult transition. The best answer of all is to quickly accept the advice that one should never eat dinner alone.

2. *Find a quiet place*—All of us have a need for quiet privacy and a degree of independence. Many students going to college today have never had a roommate growing up. They are accustomed to having their own room, accouterments, study space and bathroom. It can be an abrupt change to have to share space with one or more roommates. That is why it is important to find some place in the dorm, in a study room, in one of the academic buildings or even by periodic walks outside to find a comfortable location where one can put things into perspective and begin to assume a greater control over one's life.

None of this is to suggest that a new student should become a loner or an isolationist or someone shy around people. Rather, it is simply a reminder that all of us need a place apart where we can quietly mull over the day, think about tomorrow and just relax comfortably in our own skin.

3. *Don't be afraid to cry*—For male students, it may be especially hard to express one's emotions around people that one does not know very well. That would include new roommates, next-door neighbors, members of one's various extracurricular activities, and even residence staff and faculty. No one wants to be thought to be a cry baby or emotionally fragile or unable to cope with the reality of everyday life.

But there are moments, especially in times of transition away from home, when it simply makes sense to cry and let one's emotions burst forth. Whether that happens in public space or private space, with a good friend or a trusted counselor or walking around the campus, it is a way of getting used to expressing our emotions as young adults.

It may be surprising to discover that other people can accept you on your own terms. Many people are especially touched when someone who is young and inexperienced feels confident enough to cry in their company. It may recall for them comparable experiences in their own lives.

The important thing is that one should feel free eventually to express the whole range of emotions from hearty laughing, to stolid reaction to challenges, to weeping over some difficult information or unprecedented challenge. Crying can be good even if it is not how we want normally to be remembered.

4. *Be proud of your family*—It is always said that we do not fully appreciate how important our family has been in our upbringing before college until we get away from home. The relationship between high school teenagers and their parents is sometimes fraught with difficulty. Going through puberty is not easy and sometimes teenagers need to be apart from their family and in the presence of their friends in ways that seem challenging to parents. It is also true that parents and children can too often let each other down by how they act and the things that they say. This may be especially the case when there are multiple children in the family vying for attention.

If one's parents are able to make it to the orientation in the new college setting, it provides an opportunity to introduce your parent or parents to your new peers. It also may be an occasion for sets of parents to meet each other. One should never allow concerns about status or reputation or other relatively unimportant matters to interfere with a straightforward presentation of his or her own parents as key actors in one's own life and those to whom one is ultimately responsible.

Every family has its history, special moments, and its memories. In the end, one's family is the place where one ultimately belongs and can always be recognized by name and find a home. Except in extreme circumstances, it is important to share the pride one has in one's roots with roommates, peers, dorm staff and faculty. As the years of college go on, there will be other opportunities for all of this to be taken to the next level. There are often in residential colleges built-in opportunities for parents to return for weekends to spend time with their own children. In many ways this is a stepping-stone to the great event that is the commencement weekend.

While none of us has any say in the family that we are born into, we can surely embrace those who have brought us into the world and those that we depend upon for love, understanding and sustenance.

5. *Learn all the names*—when I was a student in college, one of my mentors taught me certain skills in remembering names of newly met individuals. His method revolved around spelling out

the name, using it multiple times on the first interaction, writing down the name when one returns to one's room and trying to work hard on remembering specific names and faces. Some people have a natural talent for this, but many other people have to work hard at it. I am convinced from my own experience that it is one of the best things we can learn in college to broaden our network of friends and to increase the chances that we will establish lifelong friendships sharing our years of study.

In this day and age where many names and faces can be found on computer data bases and in photo galleries that may be placed on bulletin boards, the skill in learning names may be less challenging than it was in years past. But most of all, it requires commitment and effort. The more people we get to know and the more names we commit to memory, the more likely it is that we will have a rich and fulfilling college experience.

6. *Don't settle for your present group of friends*—Sometimes going away to college is less challenging because one or more members of one's high school community are also present in the first-year class. There is nothing wrong with this and it can ease the transition. But it is no excuse for not taking full advantage of the much broader array of possible friends that one will encounter in a new setting. The rectors, resident assistants, and student affairs staff work hard on providing a maximum number of opportunities for people to meet each other during the first few days and weeks of school. It requires presence, attention, and responsiveness for all of this to be an asset in one's own personal life.

It goes without saying that it is important in college to reach out to people who would not necessarily be our friends and companions in our home setting. That means people of different ethnic and racial backgrounds, different religions or none, and people who have a different range of interests from our own. Athletes and musicians, those involved in student government and people who are habitués of theatre, those who like one style of music and those who like another—all of these can find a richer set of possible experiences by reaching out across the artificial boundaries that sometimes keep us apart. The same, of course, is true between men and women and those of different age groups. On some college campuses first-year students can range from those newly out of high school to people who have spent time in the military or have taken time off before beginning higher education. Whatever the differences might be, every year it will be important to try to broaden one's range of friends. This can happen in our common activities, in the social events that we attend and in the informal encounters that simply take place in the life of a busy college or university.

It is a wisdom of the ages that our present group of friends is preparatory to an ever-wider group of friends as we grow in self-knowledge, confidence and wisdom.

7. *Don't confuse your GPA with your self-worth*—During the first months of college it is often disappointing and distressing to discover that one is receiving grades that are less exemplary than what we were accustomed to in high school. For some the opposite can be the case. In any event, at the end of the first or second semester, everyone receives the grades for all of their courses and the collective grade point average that one will carry through the rest of his or her college career. For some this will be a sign of great achievement. For others, it will simply acknowledge that one is doing reasonably well. But, for a few, it will require good academic counseling and perhaps a reorientation of one's life to get back in a healthy direction academically. Every higher education institute that I am familiar with has wonderful advisors who can help deal with the anxieties of grades and occational failure. There are whole batteries of tests that one can take to help to find a better major or a more interesting direction for the future. Whatever grades one receives after the first or second semester are only an indication of how one has done up to that point. They are not determinative of the future of one's life.

8. *Get active early*—Some advisors in high school recommend that first-year students spend most of their time studying and avoid getting too much involved in extracurricular activities. There is a certain wisdom to that. However, it has been my own experience and that of many individuals that I have counseled through the years, that one also benefits from finding a range of activities that one can enjoy and that can broaden one's social world. Some people on scholarship, like athletes or people with certain academic specialties, can have much of this predetermined. Usually on college

campuses early in the first semester there is a large representative gathering of all of the potential activities in which one can get involved. It can be a bit overwhelming. But it is also a chance to think about new interests or how to make a difference during one's time at the institution. It is also possible to start your own activity if you can find enough other people who might be interested.

There probably is no magic formula but it is my suspicion that all of us have a kind of limit on how much time we can devote to productive study. What we do with the rest of our time is completely up to us. I think in the first year to have one, two or three extracurricular activities that can be fun, provide a good social opportunity and give us a chance to make a difference, can enhance our college learning rather than detract from it.

I am a big believer in activities that put us in touch with people in our community, during break time or in the summer, people who live on the margins and who have life circumstances drastically different from our own. This can be one of the most memorable moments of college when we enter into the lives of these types of individuals, not out of sympathy, but rather as a chance to learn from them, to share some of their experience and to try to be of some assistance. There are a number of nationwide organizations that have set out to promote "service learning," which suggests not only that one get involved in an outside activity off the campus but also bring that back in a reflective way into one's life in the dorm or, in a more organized way, in a classroom setting.

Higher education at its best is about helping to develop the mind, heart and spirit of the individuals entrusted to its care. A good combination of academic involvement, leadership roles and extracurricular experiences is an ideal that one could at least aspire to.

9. *Listen to alumni stories patiently*—One of the things about residential campuses is that those who have spent a significant part of their early years living in the dorm where you now reside often are motivated to come back either out of nostalgia or the desire to keep up with events on campus. This can mean that sometimes you will have visitors at unexpected hours who will want to share the news with you that they used to live in the room of the dorm where you presently reside. Inevitably, when you encounter such

individuals, they will be prone to share some of their experiences, including some of their remembered exploits and antics. It should not be surprising that amidst all of the busyness and hard work of college, in retrospect, people often remember the other sides of their college days with more immediacy.

You will be expected by them and by the institution to listen to such stories as patiently as possible. Perhaps, you can even ask questions that will give them a further opportunity to share their past with you. All of this is possible because you can have the sense that someday you will probably imitate their example and want to have open-minded, contemporary students listening to your war stories.

10. *Study, worship, socialize, exercise, serve*—If I could summarize what I would consider the best ways to take full advantage of one's four or more years of undergraduate education, these particular words would identify a set of areas of activity that ought to be a part of a full college life. *Study*, it goes without saying, is an integral part of an academic institution. Ideally, one becomes a lifelong learner and more fully responsible for one's own educational process beyond simply going to classes and labs, engaging in research projects or otherwise trying to satisfy course requirements. For those who come alive intellectually, college can be among the prized years of one's life.

For those who come from religious backgrounds, the years of college can be an opportunity for making fundamental decisions about one's own faith life. Even on secular campuses, there are plenty of opportunities for one to *participate in one's own faith tradition* whether in terms of worship, retreats or faith sharing. At religiously affiliated schools like Notre Dame, there are opportunities galore for every possible aspect for one's faith heritage to be explored. It is a shame when, for one reason or another, individuals do not take advantage of this opportunity.

Socialization is an integral part of a healthy, satisfying and happy life. Some people are more shy than others, some are more gregarious, but everyone needs good friends, loving companions and an opportunity to develop and share one's life as a person. College is great for late night conversations, the baring of one's soul to a trusted friend, and learning how to listen to the joys and struggles of others.

Everyone knows that they should *exercise* on a regular basis as well as get sufficient amounts of *sleep*. But these are two areas of contemporary higher educational life where people can fall into bad routines. Exercise can take every form under the sun from walking and running to cycling, lifting weights, or working on various aerobic exercises or participating in hall teams and various forms of intramural athletics. The important thing is to do it regularly and make it an integral part of one's life.

Finally, *service* is one of the reasons we exist in the world— that we can enter into the lives of others, especially those less privileged than ourselves, and make a difference. When this begins in college or builds on the experiences of high school, everyone benefits. One can discover one's leadership capacity in these forms of activity. Whether one is a leader, a behind-the-scenes person or a follower, all of us have roles to play. Sometimes the role can shift from one activity to the next. I had the good fortune to engage in service activities in other parts of the world in college and this helped to reorient my life. The important thing is to get involved.

Helicopter Parents

I do not know who came up with the name "helicopter parents," but it refers to a reality that many of us on undergraduate college campuses experience on a regular basis. It refers to the inability of some parents to let go, to pull back from the kind of responsibilities they bore earlier in their son's or daughter's life. Often, after orientation is completed, it is a very traumatic time for both parents and students. Occasionally, there are emotional displays at the time of departure. But, more often, it all sets in later. That is why homesickness can befall any number of students for any number of reasons. The same thing is true of parents leaving behind their most precious resource.

In this age of instant communication, where one can use the various electronic devices to stay in touch 24/7, it is not surprising that sometimes both parents and students take full advantage of this sort of regular interaction. It is understandable perhaps for a short period of time. But the longer the parental involvement remains as it was when their sons and daughters were younger, the harder it may be for both parties to pull back. When I was an undergraduate student at Notre Dame, one of my peers from Baltimore had a mother who decided to take a hotel room in downtown South Bend so that she could be available whenever her son might seek her advice. To me, at that time, this seemed somewhat comical. But it was an earlier manifestation of the same tendency. My mother on occasion, after she heard about this, would kid me that she was going to move into the area. I never took this seriously, but if she had meant it, I would have been petrified.

One of the points of pressure between parents and children is what they will study in college. In this era of pragmatic decision-making, it is not unusual for parents to want their children to take the seemingly easy path by majoring in some area of business or engineering or the medical sciences. They seem to think that there will be automatic jobs at the end. First-year academic advisors have to deal with this issue all the time. The advisor's role is to help the student find a college and major area of study that can be both doable and satisfying to the student. In college, one wants to avoid making premature decisions that seem to lay out a game plan that may not be suitable to the individual once they graduate. Despite the evidence, the most important thing is that people be happy with their major and develop a level of confidence so that, when they eventually enter the workforce, they are both well prepared and enthusiastic about pursuing their careers. Ideally, those who are studying one of the disciplines of engineering or business or architecture or the natural sciences need to have the same level of commitment and passion as those who are studying the so-called liberal arts, social sciences and the fine and performing arts.

At Notre Dame, we have a required curriculum of core courses that everyone must take no matter what their college or department mental majors might be. This is at least one way of preventing a too narrow understanding of what undergraduate education is about. One compromise between parents and children sometimes revolves around the double major—for example, one in business or economics or a branch of engineering or science and the other in one of the liberal arts or social sciences or fine or performing arts. Therefore, someone may choose to be a combined finance and psychology major or an accounting and theology major or a chemical engineering and music major.

It is more difficult for parents to influence how students' friendship patterns evolve since they do not necessarily see them on a regular basis. But when they learn names from conversations with their son or daughter, they can then go to the internet and look for information about the students that their offspring have befriended, such as their family and personal background and interests.

Too much parental intervention can be a hindrance. For hall staff and those engaged in counseling students at whatever level, it makes it more difficult for them to empower the students to become responsible for their own futures. Such advisors do not want to get into a fight over influence with parents. As a result of all of this, the best thing parents can do is trust the institution and its support services. Everyone has to make a few mistakes in order to chart a healthy path for their futures. The more parents give over responsibility to the support services of the institution and to the common good sense of those that they have brought into the world and nurtured in every possible way, the better for everyone involved.

I once saw a message on a hanging in a house that I visited that said something like "The responsibility of the parents is to give their children first deep roots and then wings." This suggests that parenting inevitably takes place in stages and the transition to college is often the beginning of another crucial stage in the dynamic between parents and children as the children move into young adulthood. In the end, over the course of time, the roles will eventually be reversed and students will become adults and will assume responsibility for their own parents as they go through the aging process. At least the parents have a good reason to hope that that will be the case. The more mature they become in college, the better prepared they will be for that later role.

Service Learning

Today, even in grade school, no less high school, students are encouraged to get involved in some form of service activity off their school grounds. Depending on the age of the students involved, this could be something as simple as visiting a nursing home or a center for the homeless or tutoring a young child or planting a garden. The intention is to broaden the perspective of the students so that they can recognize that there is a world way beyond the one that they are most familiar and comfortable with. Many of these activities do not require substantial time, although there is always the question about transportation. Sometimes parents get involved as well, either as drivers or chaperones. When these sorts of activities are well organized, they can have a real impact on the students themselves.

By the time students get to high school, the possibility exists for even more significant kinds of activity. This can mean touring around a neighborhood that is different from the one they grew up in or interviewing people involved in risky professions like police or firefighters or emergency medical crews. Perhaps the most dramatic such opportunities take place when a school organizes a trip to another part of the world, not so much as a form of tourism, but rather as a chance to experience a different culture, especially the way of life of those less fortunate than one's self. Many students that I have taught at Notre Dame have undertaken such trips in the summertime and often the experience has had a profound impact on their sense of responsibility to make the world a better place.

For years I was involved on the board and later chaired an organization called Campus Compact, which tried to promote on college and university campuses the notion of "service learning." This concept suggested that the important thing was not only to have the raw experience, but also to learn how to process it—whether by writing a report or taking a class or somehow thinking through the significance of what one had experienced.

Most colleges now have some kind of center that facilitates such opportunities for college students. Depending on the amount of time they have available to them, and what classes they are taking for credit, there is a whole array of possible types of involvement. The important thing, in my opinion, is to start with something simple and doable and build on that in each successive year of school.

Ideally, the professors of the institution will be eager to get involved in incorporating such opportunities into their own courses. For example, the seminar that I teach first-year undergraduates, which has an intercultural, international orientation, also includes a class visit to the South Bend Center for the Homeless. Before they go there and afterwards, they have a chance to hear from the directors and staff of the Center, to meet the guests and to hear some of their stories. It is one of the ways of recognizing that homelessness can happen to anyone, depending on how their life plays out. Individuals can be subject to addiction or mental illness or unexpected unemployment or a criminal record or something else that makes it difficult for them to gain and sustain employment. What the Center for the Homeless does in South Bend is to try to provide the participants in the program a capacity to rebuild their lives, to gain employment and to have independent living.

It is also possible to take one's major area of study—for example, one of the medical disciplines—and develop activities that revolve around that, like volunteering in emergency rooms, hospitals, clinics or doctor's offices. One can also do research with professors as a way of exploring how medical procedures and breakthroughs take place. Somebody interested in law could volunteer at a law office or work with the district attorney or volunteer in a judge's office. They could also spend time visiting the local court system or the jails. Students interested in entrepreneurship and the possibility of starting their own businesses could well learn from successful business leaders who took a raw idea, brought it to fruition and have developed a good workforce with excellent remuneration and safe working conditions. This could reinforce the notion that creating jobs is one of the best ways of alleviating poverty. While service and learning can take place separately in a college environment, I want to suggest that bringing them together in some organized way can maximize the learning environment of an institution. That way we can engage the minds, hearts, and the spirits entrusted to our care. In addition, they can also recognize the value of working on a common project with peers and sense the importance of organizational skills and leadership.

When I was a student, I spent three successive summers working as a volunteer in Latin America, twice in Mexico and once in Peru. This literally changed my life and my perspective about my future possibilities. Similar things have happened to other people with whom I am familiar. In each of the situations that I was involved in as an undergraduate, I also kept a diary of the experiences, which I shared with many other people, including the benefactors who had supported our engagement. This taught me how to focus on what was taking place and how to look at what I was experiencing not only in individual terms but also structurally. While I had no ready answers for the problems with poverty, unemployment, family dislocation or the other ills that I was seeing firsthand, it was important that I recognized that, while there were no quick fixes, there were steps that had been taken by others that had achieved some degree of effectiveness.

In the end, service learning is not intended to promote utopianism or naïve idealism. Rather it is trying to help students become more aware and more familiar with the highly diverse context in which people in this country and around the world live on a daily basis. Such awareness can lead to systematic reflection and the charting of reasonable efforts that one can invite advocacy. That is what service learning, at its best, entails and that is why I think it is such an integral component of a full education on our campuses.

Roommates

When I began my undergraduate career at Notre Dame, my first-year roommate was from Glen Cove, Long Island. He had originally intended to go to the Air Force Academy, but had not received a nomination. So Notre Dame was his second choice. He did reasonably well in engineering but still yearned to attend the Air Force Academy, so he quit Notre Dame thinking that his admission was assured. Unfortunately, that was not the case and, when he applied to get back into Notre Dame, he was not accepted. His name was George and we got along reasonably well most of the time. In those days we had "lights out" at a specified time each night so we often spent the wee hours of the morning talking about everything under the sun. I was sorry to see George go, but I have had no contact with him since that first year together.

My second-year roommate was a fellow basketball player

named Bill. He was six feet nine inches and about 280 pounds. He had the upper bunk and I sometimes imagined myself being crushed to death at night. With both of my roommates, I had occasional battles of one kind or another, usually over the temperature in the room or some topic that we disagreed about. Bill eventually flunked out of Notre Dame. For my junior and senior years, I had a single, which was just fine with me.

One of the big issues in dorm life these days is that many first-time college students have had not only their own room, but also their own bathroom when growing up. For them it can be somewhat startling to share a room with someone else. And yet, there is strong evidence that for first-year college students it is a lot better to have a roommate or more than one, rather than to have a single. Sharing space with someone else is a good way, in most cases, to have some kind of a social support system and someone to share one's life with.

In general, one has little choice over who one's first-year roommate might be. At least that is the case at Notre Dame. It is a lot like being born into a family since one has no say in the family of one's own origin. Every effort is made by hall staff to ease the transition and take care of any problems that might arise between or among roommates. For example, if there are four roommates, even if they share two separate bedrooms, it can turn out that three hit it off and one does not. In that case, it is important to facilitate a better dynamic with the fourth roommate. Sometimes the personality clashes are so severe that it may be necessary for someone to change roommates before the first year is finished. The roommate from hell may be entirely in one's imagination but it still brings emotional stress for those who cannot get along. The things that roommates have to come to grips with can range across the board. It could be that one snores loudly and keeps the other awake. It could be that their study times and social patterns are discrepant and one wakes the other up unnecessarily. It may be that one of the roommates is much more devoted to study than the other. It could be that they have such different value standards that one feels under attack from the other. Ideally, good roommates learn to share their life experiences with one another. This can entail simply chatting at night while lying in bed or spending social time together or seeking to find out more about the roommate's family background and cultural heritage. Sometimes the problem revolves around the parents and not around the roommates themselves. Parents may be less amenable to someone from a different religious or cultural background. They may fear the social-economic discrepancy between the two. When asked, most alumni of higher education institutions, when they reflect back on their college days, will highlight the bull sessions that they had often into the wee hours of the morning. They could have talked about everything from romantic interests, to politics, to career goals, to the local athletic teams, to financial aspirations.

As a hall staff person, when roommate problems develop, I have found it helpful to first talk to them independently. That way you can get a better sense of how the dynamic has gone and what the issues of conflict seem to be. Then, when everyone is together, you can lead the conversation in a way that may be productive. The problem may be that one or both or any of the roommates may be more candid with you than they are with each other. But that is a skill that they are going to have to learn in dealing with human conflict for the rest of their lives.

When I talk to the students that I teach, who are all first-year undergraduates, and I ask them about their roommates, they sometimes say they hardly see each other. This may be a function of what they are majoring in or the nature of their extracurricular involvements.

Some students have one expectation for a roommate with whom one shares common space and another expectation for a close personal friend that one may interact with in a variety of settings. There is nothing wrong with that.

All of us know having a roommate can be a good preparation for one's later life, especially if it entails marriage. Most of all, having a roommate, or more than one, and sharing time together in the intimate circumstances of a college dorm is a great opportunity for developing friendships that will last a lifetime. This is the hopeful result of such housing arrangements during one's undergraduate years.

Junior Parent Weekend

Both colleges and universities that have a strong residential tradition set aside a particular weekend in which they invite parents to come back and enjoy the student experience. This is intended as a reinforcement of the bonds within the family, but also a chance to experience firsthand student life in the present generation.

At Notre Dame, this tradition revolves around Junior Parent Weekend, which takes place in February. It was originally done in the middle of the sometimes-cruel South Bend winters because there wasn't that much happening on the campus. Over time, it has evolved into a huge and elaborate set of events. Almost all of the groundwork is done by juniors, assisted by sophomores eager to take a bigger role the following year. There are Student Affairs personnel that help oversee the entire operation and pass on wisdom from the past, but they deliberately try not to get involved in running meetings or telling people what to do.

From my experience Junior Parent Weekend is a wonderful chance for juniors to spend precious time with their parents and introduce them to their peer group of friends. It is also a time where roles are beginning to be reversed. At the beginning of college, it is the parents who tend to hold the primary role. Often, if the parents subsequently come back for an athletic event or some other occasion, they still are in charge. But by the time Junior Parent Weekend comes along, it is the students that are beginning to take the initiative in the relationship between themselves and their parents.

At Notre Dame, the big events are the Gala on Friday night, the Mass and dinner on Saturday night, and the concluding brunch on Sunday morning. In-between time is taken up with events in the various academic units, in the residence halls, and sometimes in common venues on the campus. At the big events, there are usually speakers, including the Junior Class President, the University President and other representatives of the class effort, including those who oversee the planning for the weekend. In my 18 years as President, I was always the celebrant of the Mass, with someone else preaching, and the main speaker at the Saturday evening dinner. Separate from that, on Friday evening there would be a big introductory fest and I would stand in one part of the arena and for three or four hours welcome the parents to the campus and usually pose for photos as well. I always saw this as an opportunity rather than a burden.

In some ways, Junior Parent Weekend (or its equivalent on other campuses) is a warm-up for commencement weekend, but with a lot less pressure. Properly executed, it is a great celebration of the sending families, of the university itself, and of all the aspirations that both groups have for the future of the students. On the Notre Dame campus, it is a huge logistical exercise. I have often said that those responsible for organizing the weekend are ready to run the world!

On my part, I look back with great fondness to all of the people that I met and the ways in which the love and pride that was manifest on the weekend was a great celebration of the highest human values and hopes for the future.

Catholic College Students

In my many years of working at the University of Notre Dame and in reading the literature about similar institutions, I have come to a number of conclusions about the challenges and opportunities that people like myself have in working with this age group. I have been involved in this activity long enough to know that each generation has distinctive qualities and issues that they deal with, but there are also many constants that can be identified that are cross-generational. At their best, contemporary college students are sensitive, bright, resilient, hard working and fun to be with. In many ways, they are much more sophisticated than my generation was. Many have traveled to other parts of the world or have had a chance to explore the riches of the United States as well. Characteristically, they are more open to differences of race, gender, sexual orientation or religion than was true in my time. They are children of the internet and have a difficult time being off-line. Electronic communication makes it possible for them to interact with their peers and family members at great distances from one another. It also allows them to have peer groups, some members of which they will never meet in person. Their sense of Church has been affected by the parish life that they have known firsthand, whether or not they went to Catholic primary and secondary schools, whether both of their parents are practicing Catholics or not. They also are aware of the sex-abuse scandals that have often rendered the voice of bishops and other Church leaders close to irrelevant. On the other hand, they are attracted to people who seem wise or holy or can help them figure out what they want to do with their lives. They relish getting together with large groups of people like themselves, for example, at World Youth Days. They also have known, sometimes firsthand, what it means to do regular live-shooter drills in their schools. Additionally, they have lived in a world where marijuana has become more and more legalized and where some of their peers may have had horrible experiences with other drug use that can be death dealing.

At their worst, contemporary Catholic students can be shallow, preoccupied with themselves, materialistic, prone to trendiness, and inconsistent from one issue to another. Like teenagers and young adults in the past, they can be very impacted by peer culture and its hollowness. Sometimes their parents make them excessively concerned about what their job prospects in the future might look like and this can have a strong influence on what course of study they follow. Many have had access to a wide range of options when it comes to what they own, wear, or utilize. When something becomes hot and popular on various internet sources, it can sweep the country quickly. This can be true about pop idols, fashion, music, dance, or any other form of human activity.

For those who minister to young Catholic college students in the American cultural context, we have a number of challenges ahead of us. For example, we can no longer presume that they possess theological literacy or a firsthand experience of the Church calendar, the cycle of feasts or a familiarity with the holy men and women of the past. From my experience as a teacher, they are eager to learn but need to know what they do not know.

Secondly, they have a strong desire for the creation of affective communities where they have a sense of belonging and where people are known by their name. In large urban parish settings or even large school environments, it is sometimes difficult for individual students to find their niche. That is why so many campus ministry groups are intent upon promoting the development of close-knit communities that pray together, sometimes socialize together, and create outreach opportunities for service.

Finally, there is a great need to help cultivate the skill of ethical deliberation. One often hears from young people the phrase "Who am I to judge," which suggests that it is inappropriate to make moral judgments about other people's values or behaviors. But, of course, this belies the issue since it is an adult responsibility to make such judgments on a regular basis. What students probably mean is that they do not wish to be judgmental in the bad sense of the term or prejudicial or biased in the way they respond to how people live in a pluralistic society. In fact, they and all of us make judgments about behavior, others and our own, on a regular basis. The challenge is how to do such judging, first of all being clear about our personal values and what is at stake, and then trying to figure out the most appropriate way to achieve what our ultimate goals are. This is especially true in matters like the relationship between love, sexuality, and personal responsibility. It is also the case in trying to think about the relationship between love and justice. Students eventually figure out that there is a difference between something being illegal and being immoral. Some behavior that is immoral from a Christian vantage point is not illegal. Some things that are illegal are not about the moral realm, but about civil behavior.

In the end, I remain optimistic and upbeat about the potential of the present generation of students to be inspired by high ideals, to be encouraged by the example of men and women of integrity and faith in their own world and in previous history, and to recognize that there are other young people who can be their allies as they seek to be the agents of reform and better possibilities for the future. All of this in the end needs to be related to our relationship to God, to our practices of prayer, including the sacraments, and to the ways in which we experience and offer mercy and forgiveness.

Reflections on Notre Dame's 175th Anniversary

Certain historical celebrations provide an opportunity for alumni(ae), contemporary students and prospective students to discover (or rediscover) the distinctive moments, challenges and leadership cadres that have allowed an institution to not only continue in existence but also to thrive. For Notre Dame, on its 175th Anniversary, I will highlight three themes: survival, aspiration, and uniqueness.

1. *Survival*—In 1842, the first problem that the founding Holy Cross religious community faced was the almost complete absence of financial resources, trained personnel, and supportive neighbors. They had been deeded the land by the Bishop of Vincennes, Indiana, and, when they arrived, they found effectively one building—a Log Chapel with some primitive housing accommodations. As a result, their first task was to build facilities, farm the land, and establish the rudimentary bases of an educational institution.

   In the 1850s, over 20 students and faculty died from cholera and yellow fever. No one was sure what the cause was but Father Edward Sorin, the first President, suspected that it had something to do with the dam that prevented the water from the two lakes from draining properly into the St. Joseph River. After Father Sorin suggested to his comrades that the dam needed to be destroyed (because the farmer who owned it would not sell), the brothers proceeded clandestinely to destroy the dam. And people stopped dying.

   In the 1860s, with the onset of the American Civil War and the need for young men to serve in the military on both sides, Notre Dame lost most of its college students but remained open because it had primary, secondary and trade schools. Its diversity of educational levels made all the difference. (Later, during the First World War, it was Army ROTC training programs, and during World War II, it was Navy training programs, that served the same purpose. Even during the Korean and Vietnam Wars, especially the latter with all of the turmoil on college campuses, Notre Dame provided a mix of academic offerings that prevented the campus from becoming depopulated.)

In 1879, after the Main Building burned to the ground (along with several adjacent buildings), Notre Dame was able to rebuild and reopen in four months when many other institutions in that period that were struck by major fires were forced to close.

Notre Dame also survived the Great Depression in the 1930s and other times of economic downturn. Even periodic debates about its religious identity or its level of aspiration did not ultimately detract from its capacity to grow and to gain in prestige and reputation.

2. *Aspiration*—Among other fine qualities, Father Edward Sorin was a visionary. In 1844, he gained approval from the State Legislature that the institution would be called the University of Notre Dame du Lac (even though in its first ten years, it never had more than 25 students, only one or two of whom were college students).

After the great fire of 1879, Father Sorin (then Superior General) was able to raise the money, not only to rebuild the Main Building but also, over time, to build a Golden Dome with a statue of Mary, Notre Dame, on the top. And this has become arguably the most recognizable symbol of any college or university in the country.

In the early part of the 20th Century, there was a debate within the governing Holy Cross community about the future path of the University. One side, represented by Fathers Corby and Morrissey, would have kept it as a regional college with earlier stages of education still available. The other side, represented by Fathers Zahm and Burns, dreamed that Notre Dame could become a distinguished university with outstanding faculty and students drawn from a wider geographical pool. Fortunately, the latter group won.

In the 1920s, as Notre Dame grew in size, it did not have sufficient residential space on campus to house an appropriate percentage of its students. So Fathers Matthew Walsh and Charles O'Donnell oversaw the construction of Howard, Lyons, Morrissey, Alumni and Dillon Halls and the South Dining Hall and the residential tradition was reestablished. And with the construction of Notre Dame Stadium in 1930, a new set of possibilities in athletics was opened up, at a scale way beyond the immediate needs of the campus.

Finally, during Father Ted Hesburgh's thirty-five years as President, Notre Dame's possibilities as a graduate and research university, as a national and international actor, and as a co-educational institution and as a place, in the wake of Vatican II, where lay talent and support was mobilized and incorporated into the governance structure, were realized.

3. *Uniqueness*—Right from its origins, Notre Dame saw itself as a Catholic institution. This flowed naturally from its founding religious community. They wore distinctive garb, lived with the students according to a French boarding school model, and expected regular religious practice.

With the completion of the second Sacred Heart Church in the 1870s, there was a center for campus worship in addition to the chapels in the residence halls. The major events of the campus calendar always had a religious dimension, especially the opening and closing of the school year as well as Christmas, Easter and holy days of obligation.

With the passage of time, the academic curriculum included courses in religion, later theology, for all undergraduates as well as philosophy and a core curriculum. Center areas of study like the Medieval Institute and later the Kellogg and Kroc Institutes, the University of Notre Dame Environmental Research Center (UNDERC) and the Center for Civil Rights and the Center for the Study of American Catholicism, all contributed explicitly to Notre Dame's Catholic identity.

With the Cedar Grove and Holy Cross Cemeteries on campus, Sacred Heart Church (later Basilica) as a center for weddings and baptisms and funerals, the Grotto of Our Lady of Lourdes as a center of prayer and devotion, the custom of gathering for prayer for special events, and the prevalence of religious indoor and outdoor art, the religious atmosphere of Notre Dame has indeed been pervasive. (For me, the Mass on the South Quad on September 11, 2001, and the multiple Masses in the aftermath of the Women's Swim Team accident were particularly noteworthy in this regard.)

After 175 years of existence, we at Notre Dame have much to be thankful for. Those who live, study and work here now are inheritors of a grand tradition.

Succeeding a Legend

I had the rather unusual experience of succeeding as President of Notre Dame one of the most iconic and legendary figures in American higher education, the Reverend Theodore M. Hesburgh, C.S.C., who had served as President of Notre Dame for 35 years. Father Ted, as he liked to be called, took Notre Dame into the 20th century and beyond. He was a successful fundraiser, an advocate for Catholic higher education, and a trusted confidant of presidents and popes. He was responsible in many ways for some of the civil rights legislation and he also interacted on a regular basis with Russian scientists during the Cold War. Fr. Ted was a theologian by formal education, but was always interested in a wide variety of topics and was a quick read. In any case, it is fair to say that many people wondered if I would be up to the challenge when I succeeded him.

Since this was a question that I was asked not only in my first year as president, but 18 years later when I stepped down, I have thought a lot about transition in leadership not only in higher education but in just about every walk of life.

The first thing I would say is that I inherited a university that was in good shape and had a lot of momentum. One of my first responsibilities was to make sure that I didn't misdirect its energies while I was seeking to articulate what I thought the future possibilities looked like. All of this took place as a kind of collective effort with consultation that was broad across other administrators, the faculty, the Board of Trustees and the various Advisory Councils, the student body, and the alumni groups. When a new president, or other major leader, takes over they have, if they are lucky, a period of time in which new relationships can be established and new ideas explored. Some presidents have not been as lucky as I was and they inherit institutions that have been mismanaged or have severe financial challenges or do not have the right mix of people in central leadership positions. It becomes imperative then that the new leader first address questions about the leadership team and strategies for seeking financial health. This might entail making some dramatic decisions, but this will be something that everyone is looking in on to see whether the new leader has the courage to take such action.

All things being equal, it is important to have the support of the out-going president. There may be some circumstances where this is not possible when one is taking over after a scandal or financial crisis or some other situation that has discredited the previous president. But, if it is possible, it is important to celebrate the contributions of the out-going president and to keep a good relationship going into the future. Many members of the Board of Trustees who were involved in the selection process will defer to the out-going president when it comes to evaluating the new president as time unfolds. Secondly, it is important that the governing board, whatever title it might go by, recognize their responsibility to support the new leader in every way possible. This is true not only in the first year, but also in succeeding years through the term of the original contract. In a sense, both the board and the leadership group are in it together. They should be in regular contact, particularly in the interaction between the president and the board chair, and offer frank and respectful evaluations of what needs to be done and respond to any new proposals.

It is also important for the new president to have one or more individuals who report directly to him or her. This is one of the ways of sharing some of the responsibility of the office, being represented at meetings that one cannot attend, and hearing things that people will be reluctant to tell you. A good executive assistant can be invaluable. And, depending on the scale of responsibilities, it may be appropriate to have multiple assistants whose primary task is to assist the work of the president directly.

Finally, it is important for the new president to establish a kind of rhythm in the job that allows the individual sufficient time for relaxation and refreshment. There is a great danger in the first year in office to be on the go non-stop and to put one's own health at risk. Before I took over as president, I went around and consulted with other sitting presidents and one of the best bits of advice I got was to try to get enough sleep and exercise. Both of these are important in the long run. And, for someone like myself, it was essential to make sure I attended to my discipline of prayer and interaction with my local religious community. For married presidents, the same would hold when it comes to the dynamic with one's spouse and children. They can fully understand how a new job requires a particular deep investment of time but this can too easily lead in the wrong direction. Leaders are ultimately human beings and everything we know about the make-up of healthy individuals is that they determine what kind of mix they need to not only persist in their responsibilities, but to thrive in the face of them.

Leadership as a CEO of an organization can be an energizing and fulfilling way of giving one's life in the service of others. It can also be fun, at least some of the time. If one feels pervasively burdened by the job, it is predictable that one will not have a long term of service. Successful transitions are necessary for the institutions that are undergoing them. Everybody has a vested interest in seeing the new president succeed.

OCCASIONAL MUSINGS

In this final section, I draw upon my life and experiences to offer a few isolated reflections on topics that struck my fancy.

The Power of Words

One of the things that distinguishes human beings from other forms of life is our capacity to communicate. As we grow older and develop a vocabulary and as we are exposed to words and their various formats, we become more capable of expressing our wants, desires, and dreams as fundamental human feelings. Our use of words and language is a constant reminder of our deep social rootings. Most of us learn a distinctive language, like English, and hopefully we become more adept in utilizing it for all the purposes of everyday life. In school, on television, in movies and in other fora, we eventually become exposed to individuals who have a great capacity to use words with style and creativity. People who are fluent in multiple languages usually discover that there are certain distinctive words in each of the languages they know that are not easily translated into the other. Many of us learn specialized vocabulary as part of our work situation or neighborhood slang or interests we have like sports or music or one of the other performing arts. English has the largest vocabulary of any language that I am familiar with because it constantly adopts terminology from other languages, sometimes because of the influence of people who come from backgrounds where the other language is the coin of the realm. One of the best arguments for studying Latin and Greek is that they are so decisive in the structure of English vocabulary. So many prefixes and suffixes are derived from the classic languages. The more familiar we are with these building blocks of words, the easier it is to make sense of unfamiliar terminology.

When I was a boy, I was always a big reader. They used to have a contest for Catholic grade schools and they would give an award to students who had read the most books each month. I was the perennial winner at St. Anthony's grade school. One of the techniques I learned was that, when I came across an unfamiliar word, I'd underline it and later go back and look it up in the dictionary and try to use it in conversations so I not only would become more familiar with its meaning but I could make it part of my active vocabulary as well. Later on, when I was in college, I found that there were books that one could buy in order to develop a larger and more effective vocabulary. Usually they included fun quizzes to gauge how one was doing. I used to keep a list of words that I had incorporated into both my passive and active vocabularies and, when I looked back at the end of my college career, I was amazed at how familiar all the words were to me at that point.

For many people swear words seem to be the fill-ins when you can't think of what else to say. Many people have commented that people whose everyday vocabulary is the most limited often swear characteristically. It is as if they can make their point only by being shocking rather than by finding an appropriate and nuanced word or phrase. One of the great risks today is that the overwhelming reliance on various forms of electronic communication, which often use shortcuts, is the potential for a kind of homogenization in communication. People may lose an appreciation for the capacity of some poets, novelists, and playwrights to explore the richness of the human condition through the words that they generate and the phrases that they use creatively. Every individual may have insights of his or her own, but they are always private until one develops the capacity to express what is in one's mind and heart.

Eloquent orators, captivating songwriters, and insightful novelists are all ready to share their gifts with the rest of the human community. They become, in a sense, part of the human effort to find effective ways to say what is on our minds, to probe our interior wants and desires and to imagine the extent of human possibilities. Newspaper, magazine and book editors have the common responsibility to make sure that high standards are maintained with regard to the official roles that they play in recognizing and rewarding the most talented communicators in our midst. The same is true with book critics and those who employ the various forms of media to interpret trends as well as positive and negative directions in contemporary culture.

In Christian life, we use the word *logos*, which is the Greek terminology for "word," to describe Jesus of Nazareth. We say he is the Word come down from heaven who through his teaching, preaching, prophetic and healing ministries became the human embodiment of the living God. Theologians, catechists, preachers and others entrusted with this Word have a huge responsibility to communicate this message with appropriate levels of respect and attention. While our own words, theories, and forms of expression are always inadequate to the Word of God, we are entrusted with the task of trying to make it comprehensible to people of our own day and history.

In the end, we are inevitably people of words. The challenge is to become more attuned to the power of words as forms of human expression both as speakers and listeners.

Leadership

In my eyes, leadership is ultimately about people, people, people. It involves recruiting, hiring, or otherwise attracting to a common work those who are committed, well prepared and properly motivated. Leadership at any level, whether in higher education, business life, government, the Church, not-for-profit organizations or whatever, begins with this recognition—that people are at the heart of the activity and people are the ones that the leader has primary responsibility for. People are more important than strategic plans, budgets, fund raising, the issuing of reports and community relations. In more complex endeavors like the modern college or university, the leader is usually selected by the governing board. The person is then entrusted with responsibilities for every activity of the institution. This means that one needs to be surrounded by a talented coterie of people who will oversee the particular rounds of endeavor within the institution. One of the primary tasks of a leader is to assure that the right mix of people are present in these next level leadership positions and that they are working together toward a common goal. This can be achieved only with the right mix of one-on-one meetings, gatherings of the whole group and external outreaches by different combinations of the leadership group. If this goes well, the leader can have greater confidence that all the sub-units of the institution will adopt a similar model. It is usually necessary to begin the year with a several-day meeting so that the leadership group can look back on the previous year and evaluate how things went, make appropriate recommendations for change and then turn one's attention to the future. This sort of endeavor, which ideally also includes some relaxed time together, can spark the level of enthusiasm that everyone has for the coming year.

It is often said that meetings are the bane of contemporary administration. Meetings are inevitable for any group but, if they are properly prepared for and well executed, then people can see that they have an important purpose in the common life. The big challenge is to create types of meetings that are the right combination of presentations about particular issues and group conversation trying to come toward some sort of consensus. For example, in putting together the budget for the coming year it is necessary to have all of the proper information before one discusses alternative directions, whether that be cutting back in some area of activity or taking on a new set of challenges.

When it comes to looking for new members of the central administrative team or others who carry heavy responsibility, I have mixed feelings about the use of search firms. Most institutions of whatever kind use search firms at least some of the time. They are expensive, but it can be a good way of broadening the range of potential candidates and doing a lot of the groundwork ahead of time. However, there are occasions when doing a search through internal resources, particularly for institutions that have a particular and distinctive identity, may be more satisfactory in the end.

A leader's efforts at motivating a new workforce can take many forms. Some are good at oratory and making live or videotaped presentations in order to maximize the impact. Others are better in written statements that can be well prepared and both precise and well articulated. Sometimes symbolic events are even more effective motivators. This could include celebrating the achievements of well-known individuals or those further down in the imaginary pecking order so that everybody feels that their contribution is important. Some of these events can revolve around historical moments when the institution can look back in appreciation of those who were the initiating group for the venture. Every leader needs to make sure that there are appropriate measures of accountability for everybody in the workforce, from one's closest associates to those who are the newly hired. There are a variety of ways of engaging in this sort of activity but it is essential that these evaluation systems be consistent, fair and well respected. Ideally, there should be some outcome connected to positive and negative evaluations. In my experience, one of the hardest things about being a leader is passing on negative feedback to those who merit it. Maybe the hardest thing of all is to fire someone for incompetence or illegal activity or a lack of inspiration in one's responsibilities. On the other hand, there is nothing more satisfying than being able to promote people for a job well done.

Leaders are usually the face of the organization. I know that when I served as President of Notre Dame, I was the chief administrator, a priest representative of the founding religious community, and someone who was involved in the teaching mission and in residential life. This combination of factors gave me, and others doing similar things, a kind of distinctive face in the eyes of our multiple constituencies.

There are some leadership positions that are more difficult because it is not so obvious how to determine when things have been well done. For example, the rector of the dormitory has, at face value, responsibility for the well-being of all the students who reside there. But there is an inherent expectation that they will be able to step in to comfort the afflicted, to deal with sickness and death in the family, to confront people's misbehavior to help them grow up faster, and to oversee the physical plant. Not everyone is good at all of these activities simultaneously. The best rectors are those who keep their enthusiasm alive after years of being involved in this challenging work. They become the gurus and the wise representatives of a tradition with the passing of time. They can help new practitioners avoid some common mistakes and not be overwhelmed by events. I used to say to the new Student Government leaders elected in the spring that they needed to have a clear sense of what they wanted to try to achieve during their one year of leadership because inevitably, when they finished and the new group ran for office, they would talk about how little had been done and how much they had promised to improve things for the future. This campaigning rhetoric did not do justice to what their predecessors had achieved and all of the hard work that had gone into it. That is why they needed to have an early sense of what concrete steps they would like to be able to take to impact the well-being of the campus.

Insofar as colleges and universities have a responsibility to prepare the next generation of leaders, it is some combination of concrete extracurricular activities, reflection and book knowledge that can allow strong leaders to emerge. I think that there are some individuals who are by native talent just natural leaders. They seem to have good instincts and an attractive way of interacting with people. But there are many others who can become leaders in their own right by simply allowing themselves to get involved in various levels of responsibility. One level of satisfactory leadership can lead to higher levels of responsibility as time goes on.

Let me mention three leaders whom I hold in high regard for different reasons. President Abraham Lincoln is one of my heroes. The 16th President of the United States kept the nation together during the extremely bloody years of the American Civil War. He also effected significant change with the Emancipation Proclamation, which banned slavery within the United States. This was the beginning step toward a closer realization of the Constitutional principles that our nation had so unfortunately neglected prior to the Civil War. One of the things I most admire about Lincoln is that he changed his mind so often on the basis of his concrete experience. When you visit the Lincoln Memorial in Washington D.C. and you see some of his most famous addresses inscribed on the walls and then you see him sitting in the chair, looking out over the mall toward the Washington Monument, it is a very powerful way of expressing our nation's thankfulness to him. A second leader I hold in high regard is Nelson Mandela who, despite all of the years he spent in prison during the apartheid regime in South Africa, when he was elected president he became someone who facilitated reconciliation and a new set of practices across racial and other boundaries. Instead of being vindictive and angry, he surprised everyone during his years as president when he envisioned a new set of possibilities for his country. The last leader is Sister Mother Teresa of Calcutta who founded a religious community of women and who was able to have them undertake ministry to some of the poorest and least supported of all the people, initially in India, but later in other parts of the world as well. What I admire about Mother Teresa's leadership, now St. Teresa, is that she was able to put together a structure for her religious community that has succeeded well after her own death. I have visited her sisters in various parts of the world, including Haiti, Kenya and various parts of the United States, where they administer to some of the more forsaken and least appreciated individuals with great devotion and love. Mother Teresa is the kind of leader who has left behind not only a great personal legacy, but also one of institutional structure that preserves her original vision.

In a sense leadership is a calling, an opportunity, a way of making a difference in the world. It is also a chance to pay back all of those individuals who have been generous in affecting our lives positively at earlier stages of our own personal histories.

Lessons for Life

Looking back on my life, I recognize how influenced I was by my career as an athlete. Other people could comparably point to participation in an orchestra or a theatre group or student government or a student newspaper or a not-for-profit endeavor. By getting involved in a variety of formats and playing a sequence of different roles, all of us can learn skills that will be helpful later in our lives. I like to point to four values that can be learned from such engagements.

First is the relationship between *discipline* and *asceticism*. Early in our lives, by getting involved in extracurricular activities, we can learn the fundamentals of a particular activity or practice. The same way that we can seek to master the ABC's, we can also recognize our capacity to learn other skills little by little. In some senses of the term, practice does make perfect. My greatest skill as a basketball player revolved around long-distance shooting. The attainment of a degree of confidence and skill did not come automatically. But over time, I learned how to embrace habits of excellence and to practice, practice, practice.

Discipline can lead to a kind of asceticism where we learn how to focus on certain things and give up the pursuit of others. Great athletes, musicians, artists, and public speakers all need to learn how to set their priorities and forsake what otherwise might be realistic options.

A second set of related skills has to do with the relationship between *teamwork* and *community*. In both cases, we recognize that many of the most important human activities are engaged in collaboratively. By fostering coordination and collaboration among the participants in a common activity, we can achieve a greater level of success. It is a way of focusing many gifts toward one common goal. It is also the case that we can discover strength in numbers, that is, what we could never achieve in solitary splendor we can come close to realizing by being part of a collective endeavor.

A third area of relationship among things to be learned is the relationship between *perseverance* and *fortitude*. We know as we grow older that obstacles in life are inevitable. Even some of our smoothest areas of participation can have snags. But we can also learn from our mistakes. Over time, we can realize that we can become adept in resiliency through adaptation in the face of limitations of one kind or another.

Injuries and misfortunes can test us on occasion. Many people who have tried out for a team or a particular leadership role have discovered, in retrospect, that a failure in one area of life can lead to success in others.

Finally, there is an integral relationship between the role that *mentors* play and the later role that all of us play in *passing on* what we have learned from those who have schooled us earlier in our lives. The best teachers are committed to nurturing the uniqueness of each person and group entrusted to their care. This includes trying to be inspirational and to hold our students accountable for their performances.

There are many lessons that we can learn in the course of our life and in retrospect. The important thing is, at least periodically, to review the various stages of our life and recognize what aspects of our experiences are most beneficial and attempt to always incorporate them into our present and future involvements.

Water

Water constitutes 71% of the earth's surface. However, only 2.5% of the earth's water is fresh. Of this fresh water, 1.2% is surface water and about 30% is ground water. At present utilization rates, 50% of the available fresh water is used on a regular basis—70% of this is for agricultural and sanitation and 10% for domestic uses. Most of the rest of the water in the world is salt and it lies in the ocean and connecting waterways.

Many have suggested that water is the most important of all natural resources, way more important than oil, coal, gas, and other natural fuels. Recently, Cape Town, South Africa has been dealing with the possibility, in a large metropolitan area, that they could run out of access to fresh drinking water. This of course would be devastating, not only there, but also in other contexts. We know that with climate change certain parts of the world are going through rather dramatic challenges with regard to their access to water and its implications for agriculture and human life. On the other hand, another impact of climate change is the melting of the polar icecaps with the raising of sea levels rather dramatically with all of its implications for so many port cities and regions that are adjacent to the coastline. So on one hand we have a dilemma with not enough water and, on the other hand, with too much water. Trying to find a balance between these two realities is part of what policymakers have to deal with. Approximately 780 million people do not have access to clean and safe water. As a result, they live on the boundaries of a safe and healthy life.

Living as I do in Indiana near Lake Michigan, one of the five great American lakes, I am very aware of what a great resource they are for the Midwestern part of the country. Some politicians have proposed through the years that the residents of the Great Lakes region should sell water to other parts of the country as a way of increasing the realities of financial support for urban environments. But most people, including myself, think this is a terrible idea. For many people on a regular basis and for others on trips and vacations, regular access to clean, drinkable water is gained through bottled water, provided either in glass or plastic containers. But then, this entails another ecological problem—plastic containers in particular are one of the more problematic items to be found in the oceans and seas of the world.

We are warned, not only of the shrinking of the polar icecaps, but also by other examples like the almost-disappearance of the Aral Sea in Asia, which used to be a great provider of food, water and tourism for that region of the world. Now, through over-utilization, it has shrunk to a mere reminder of its former prominence. Water is essential for human life. An individual human person can go much longer without food than without water. That is why it has been seen historically as one of the great gifts from God. Now we are coming to a greater recognition of our responsibility to preserve our natural resources, including water, for future generations. Notre Dame is especially fortunate because we lay atop a giant aquifer and we can, with the right principles of protection, have access to plentiful supplies of clean water for perhaps centuries ahead. Let us hope that with the right worldwide conversation we can be wise stewards of the clean water available to us and build a consensus about how to share access to such an important resource.

Gambling as a Social Practice

Human beings have gambled in one form or another back into our distant history as a race. In some ways it responds to our competitive urge. In many instances, it is simply a way that friends enliven their time together, whether over a card game, or a favorite team competing in a big game, or putting a few dollars down each month for lotto, or some other form of state-supervised gambling.

It is estimated that, in 2013, Americans lost $119 billion in gambling in one form or another. This means that even though there were some winners, the vast majority of those who participated lost their money to other people like themselves, or to illegal forms of betting, or at some casino, or to state-sponsored forms of competitive gambling.

The two main forms of contemporary gambling with any dollar significance are sports betting and casino-sponsored betting. The amount bet on the annual National Football League Super Bowl has been rising with each passing year. In 2016, it was somewhere near $132 million but, by 2017, it had risen to $138 million. It is estimated that the amount wagered online, on sports worldwide, is in the significant billions of dollars. In 2012, it was estimated at $74 billion. In the same year, in Nevada, $3.5 billion was wagered. The other significant form of gambling in the United States is based in casinos of one kind or another. For many years Nevada, particularly Las Vegas and Reno, had a monopoly. But in recent years, often under the sponsorship of various Native American tribes, the number of casinos has grown exponentially. In 2015, the various casinos in the United States made $18 billion and, in 2017, an estimated $19 billion. The leading casino in the United States (Las Vegas Sands) made $11 billion in 2016. As of 2014, there were 510 commercial casinos in the United States and the number has grown dramatically since then. Even in my home state of Indiana, there are now 14 casinos as of 2018.

For just about everybody who participates, gambling is a losing proposition. Some may gamble simply because it brings excitement into their life or it may provide hope for some financial windfall or it may be something that one begins to be addicted to as a form of personal activity.

The summer between my junior and senior years of college, I spent a month living in Las Vegas with the family of one of my classmates and holding a small job in a local restaurant. The two of us, plus another Notre Dame student, spent most evenings touring around the various casinos, sometimes to enjoy the entertainment, but most of the time simply to watch people lose money. With the advice of the husband of the family, I learned how to win on the nickel slots. (This was the era before they had computer chips that could follow just about anybody's habits and adjust the payout accordingly). I learned that the slot machines in the so-called inner city of Las Vegas were intended for relatively low-income people, which surely included myself. Through a disciplined way of approaching the slots, I was able to finish the summer with about $150 surplus on the nickel slots. At the same time, I could watch people simply throwing their money away, often playing five adjacent machines simultaneously, which assured that they would not finish the evening on a positive note. In those days the machines were designed so that, when somebody won a jackpot, the lights flashed and the machines made noises and there was a strong reinforcement of the expectation that the other people would soon be winners themselves. Out in the casinos that attracted the upper-class gamblers, I watched huge sums of money simply being squandered. There were a few people who played backgammon and black jack and craps and roulette. There were those who simply saw it as a form of entertainment using their discretionary income. These individuals would set a certain amount of money aside and play until it ran out. But in many of the rest, there was a sense of desperation as their resources began to dwindle. While I was there I also learned that if someone became too competitive (by counting cards), for example in black jack, the casino would politely have them leave. They were not in it to lose money.

For a period I co-chaired the NCAA Committee on Gambling. We were interested in trying to prevent, through appropriate legislation, the national opportunity to gamble in a legal way on high school and college sports. We were not concerned about what happened with the professional games. Unfortunately, we learned about how many vested interests there were in preserving both legal and illegal online gambling. We also reviewed periods of time in which various college sports had been touched by people throwing games for financial reward. Initially, this was prevalent in basketball because people could salve their consciences by losing relative to the point-spread, but winning the game. Later on, this sort of effort to rig the outcome began to spread to other sports as well.

Separate from the issues related to addiction, I would like to highlight three negative dimensions of organized gambling. First, it fosters a competitive view of reality. Gambling is often a zero-sum game in which only one or very few competitors win in the end. This fosters a view of everyday life that has many negative connotations. The second negative dimension is that it strips persons of their inherent freedom because they become a plaything of forces that are usually better organized than themselves. The development of various forms of computer technology have allowed casinos to ramp up the profits to the detriment of the fun component of those who participate. Finally, it falsifies the context of human benevolence in charity. When state-run lottos and other forms of indirect taxation spread their influence, it is often justified as a way of balancing the budget or devoting the money to one kind of good cause or another. However, there are much more direct ways in which the money that is devoted to the cause can be concentrated where it belongs. All forms of such state-sponsored activity are inherently expensive and many people take their share before the money goes to its allotted purposes.

Whether one chooses to gamble or not, especially in organized settings like casinos or online, it is important to be reflective about one's other responsibilities to family, friends, not-for-profit organizations, and other places where the same amount of money would lead to much better results for everybody involved. Much of human gambling is trivial and morally unimportant. But, in some cases, it leads to patterns of behavior or to a kind of social practice that can have horrible impacts on the individual and all of the other people that depend on the individual for support of one kind or another.

The Weather

Most of my friends think that I am somewhat nuts in that my favorite type of weather is hot and humid, like summer in Washington D.C. on August 15th. Of course, it depends on what you are wearing and what your duties are. I grew up in a household that did not have air conditioners and barely had a fan or two, so I often woke up in the morning with sweat on my body. That just seemed normal.

Having lived in South Bend, Indiana. for much of my adult life, I have accommodated to the reality of four seasons, especially harsh winters. That doesn't mean that I have to like them but I have adopted practices that minimize the harm. That means that I keep my head covered as well as my hands and feet. When I walk around the campus in the wintertime, I usually alternate between indoors and outdoors. That way I can get my exercise but do not get extremely cold. I am a big believer in an outer jacket with a hood that lies over my stocking cap when I walk around outdoors. This is especially helpful when there is a stiff wind blowing.

I can fully appreciate the beauty of spring with the beginning of the blossoming of flowers and trees and the wonder of nature. On the Notre Dame campus, this is especially appreciated if we have had a severe winter. The campus basically comes alive and, once the grass is green and everything is blossoming, it is a delight to simply walk around and appreciate the wonder of nature. I also enjoy the transition to fall when the leaves begin to change color and eventually the trees are barren. I could take winter if it only lasted a week or two because we would have a taste of snow and then it would melt quickly and we could get back to spring.

I was on the Notre Dame campus in the winter of 1977-78 when we had a total of 172 inches of snow, with 72 inches in one big storm. The campus was closed for five full days and driving was prohibited in St. Joseph County. This was the worst, but there have been a number of other winters that came close.

The nice thing about living on a college campus is that the buildings are heated and it is simply a matter of surviving outdoors until you get to your next indoor location.

In my travels, I have been in desert environments where it gets up to 135 or 140 degrees Fahrenheit. It is essential that you have sufficient amounts of water because it is easy to die of thirst if you get isolated. I spent a full year in Jordan, Minnesota, and we had 30 days of below-zero weather and I remember one day it got down to -35 degrees Fahrenheit. That degree of cold is equally challenging. You have to make sure that you are not in an environment where you can get lost, like at a ski resort.

I am a big fan of the Weather Channel. I especially check in when I have a trip upcoming or if there is a threat of dangerous weather in our area. They also cover hurricanes, tornados, floods, earthquakes and other natural disasters with a real skill. It serves their purposes to always exaggerate what the risks are when a storm is approaching so that they can maximize their audience. Most of the meteorologists that work for the Weather Channel like to be out in the field in a hurricane with the wind whipping around them and obviously finding it difficult to talk into a microphone. It is a way of personalizing what everybody else there is going through.

I was once in the eye of a hurricane in Washington D.C. It was barely hurricane force since it had come on land, but it was the eeriest phenomena to have a raging storm and then the sun and utter peace, followed by a recurrence of the heavy winds and rain. I have been in tremors related to earthquakes, but never have born the full brunt of a certified earthquake as such. I have been within 20 or 30 miles of tornados but, thank God, have never seen a tornado anywhere near where I was staying. Once we were driving in Florida and I saw a tornado in the far distance and it was scary enough. When I was in Minnesota at our Novitiate, I saw the impact of a major flood that came a mile and a half up to our property. I then had a chance, when it receded, to see the kind of damage that a flood can do. Another time I was flying near St. Louis after a flood of the Mississippi River and I could see from the air what a broad swath of land the flood had affected. Nature is often beautiful and inspiring. It has been written about by poets and novelists and mystics. But at its worst, the weather can threaten our safety and well-being to the nth degree. We need rain, but not too much. We enjoy sunny skies and beautiful puffy clouds, but fear thunderclouds and heavy winds and lightning. We enjoy rivers and lakes and swimming at the oceanside, but sometimes we have to fear when the water rises too high and the tidal flows become destructive.

I think the evidence is clear that our use of fossil fuels has had an impact, sometimes in a severe way, on our climate worldwide. We are now experiencing more severe weather events like hurricanes, floods, droughts, tornados and other natural disasters. Because we have a natural desire to live in forested areas or along the seacoast or on the sides of rivers and we often plant crops close to the water due to the need for irrigation, our very well-being can be suddenly jarred when natural disasters strike us.

Weather is simply one of the components of the natural world that we inhabit. Good weather is always a blessing. Bad weather can be tolerated except when it gets to extremes. Let us hope that we can prepare better for the kind of devastating impact that weather can sometimes have on all of us, particularly the poor who have so few resources to rebuild. We can be thankful for the courage of the Coast Guard, the Forest Service, the Air Force pilots that fly into the eyes of hurricanes, and all of those who prepare themselves to be first responders to people facing the worst of what nature can deliver. In a literal sense we are all in this together and we need to have good policies and effective responses to situations that bad weather sometimes can lead to. I hope that our government and all the governments of the world can be poised to step in, in the wake of natural disasters, to help people put their lives back together again.

I admire advanced skiers, water surfers, desert trekkers and paragliders. I hope they have fun. But, as I grow older, I figure I have had enough excitement in my life. Now, I simply want to enjoy good weather and minimize the impact of weather patterns that threaten my safety (and that of other human persons).

Airline Travel

I recently discovered that I am coming up on two million miles on United Airlines. That doesn't count mileage that I have garnered on other major airlines, as well as the Notre Dame plane and other private planes that have been rented in an emergency. That means that I have spent much of my adult life flying from one place to another. I am in many ways a fearless flyer, particularly in comparison to my experiences on highways that are foggy or rain-splattered or when you are driving directly into the sun. The quality of the technology available today, the high level of training of the pilots and the skill of the air traffic controllers all make for a high level of confidence on my part.

That does not mean that I have not had some close brushes with disaster. Twice I was flying into Teterboro Airport in New Jersey on the Notre Dame plane when we encountered unexpected problems. On one occasion it was wind shear and, on the other, we were the last plane in during a blizzard and we went off-line and turned sideways simultaneously. Fortunately, our pilots at the time, who had trained on Navy aircraft carriers, were up to the task and we landed safely. These events happen so quickly that you hardly have time to be afraid before it is all over. Another time, I was on a plane across the Pacific that fell maybe 1,500 to 2,000 feet unexpectedly and, at other times, I sweated out landing in conditions with very low ceilings. I remember one flight from Japan to California where we had bumps almost the whole trip because there was a series of fronts approaching the West Coast of the United States. Twice I have landed in Portland, Oregon, to find an ambulance and paramedics there as they took off passengers that had serious illnesses that they were afraid might be some contagious virus. As a result, we had to leave our name and address with the authorities so that we could be contacted if they decided that we were at risk. One time I was taking off from O'Hare on a flight to the West Coast and we were just about off the ground when a man nearby started yelling out "Help me. Help me." I looked around and it wasn't clear what was wrong with him but a flight attendant got up and went back to his seat. Pretty soon, they paged whether there were any physicians on the plane and they discovered there was at least one. He determined that the gentleman suffered from emphysema and had had a breathing attack. Once they gave him oxygen, his condition disappeared and we were able to continue on to our destination.

I once was given the opportunity to fly a 767 simulator at the Boeing plant in Washington. It was a fun thing to do since the cockpit goes through all of the motions that you might experience on an actual flight. When I was in charge as the purported pilot, we eventually crashed. It was simply a reminder that I didn't have either the training or the innate skill to pilot a major airliner. In the early days with the Notre Dame plane, which was a Cessna 310 and did not have air pressure, we were restricted on how high we could go and sometimes we ended up in the middle of storms. Since we had only a single pilot and I was the only passenger, I used to read the instructions in the back of the seat in front of me that said something like "If the pilot is incapacitated, please read this manual." At times it motivated me to think about taking flying lessons but I never got around to it. Now the Notre Dame plane is a jet that requires two pilots and so the same fears don't exist. Although like all passengers, I feel inconvenienced when my flights are delayed or canceled, in my more rational moments, I can recognize that that is a far better decision than taking off and finding that the plane is inoperable. Sometimes the weather we would encounter along the way would justify not taking off. On other occasions, it may be a problem in the air traffic control system or in the landing approaches at the airport at our destination. When flying into the Rocky Mountains and landing at one of the smaller airports there, the wind can be a real negative factor. That is why it always needs to be up to the pilots to determine whether or not we can land at the assigned airport.

Having spent so much time in the air, I am utterly surprised when I sit next to a passenger who has never been in an airplane before. For them it is usually a matter of either sheer panic or sheer delight. In any case, when I find out their situation, I try to comfort them with what I have learned in all of my years as a passenger. But as all of us discover inevitably, once one is up in the air, it is necessary to land somewhere. One time I was on a rented airplane and I was supposed to land in South Bend, but they were going through some maintenance on the devices and we needed to land when the ceilings were low. In addition, neither of the pilots had ever landed in South Bend before. We made two passes but were way wide of the runway, so a little while later we had to land in Elkhart, Indiana, which is not that far away and was not covered in the same level of fog that the South Bend airport was. While the pilots were reflecting about our options, we were reminded that all airplanes need to land someplace eventually.

I indeed prize what I have been able to do and see as a result of the speed and efficiency of modern aviation. It has shortened the time and distance between continents and peoples and has allowed me to explore the world in a relatively comfortable fashion. For that, I am grateful.

Washington, D.C., My Hometown

I was born in 1941 at Georgetown Hospital on May 3rd. Later my parents gave birth to my two sisters, Joanne and Mary. Right from the start, we lived within the city limits. My parents, after they moved to D.C. from Scranton, Pennsylvania, resided for a while on North Capital Street. Then, they moved to an apartment at 808 Taylor Street NE, not far from Catholic University. Finally, our family home became part of a tri-plex on 13th Street NE, near Providence Hospital.

My father's job as a Claims Adjuster for the Transit Company took him all over the metropolitan area as he interviewed various individuals involved in accidents. As a result, he became quite familiar with the D.C. area and all the intricacies of its road system. As I grew older, I became familiar with various streetcar and bus routes so that I could get around the city on my own. My father had a company car so I could only use it when he was present. That meant that before I went off to college I never had a car of my own. Nevertheless, I was a big walker and, once I got to a neighborhood, I tended to learn it from simply making my way around the various streets and alleyways. My father was a ready tour guide for family members and others who wanted to go on explorations of the city. Through his influence, I became, in subsequent years, a tour guide myself for Notre Dame classmates and various visitors that I knew from other circumstances.

Washington is an inherently beautiful city from my perspective. Because there is a height limit on the construction of buildings, it tends not to be overwhelmed by high-rises in the central government and business district. With the Potomac River separating it from northern Virginia and the Anacostia River separating one part of Northeast Washington from the other, there are many water views available. Almost all of the government buildings, from the Capitol to the Washington Monument to the White House, are available to ordinary citizens at various times of the week. And, even more importantly, the multiple component units of the Smithsonian Institute make all of their marvelous holdings, displays, and artifacts available for free. Countless times our family visited the Zoo, which is a Smithsonian-sponsored center, as well as the National History Museum, the various art galleries and later the Aerospace Building. In the summers, there were free band concerts on the steps of the Capitol, at the Jefferson Memorial, and at the Watergate section along the Potomac River.

The great Mall between the Capitol and the Washington Monument, and on to the Lincoln Memorial, was often the site for patriotic displays like the Fourth of July fireworks and various folk representations and music as well as gatherings of citizens for one purpose or another. When I was growing up in the city, I felt like there was always something interesting going on somewhere in the downtown area.

In addition to what was available close at hand, our family would take full advantage of visiting various Civil War battlefield sites like Gettysburg, Manassas/Bull Run, Fredericksburg, and Harper's Ferry. We also used to make periodic trips to Arlington National Cemetery, especially on Memorial Day, as well as Mount Vernon, where there was entrance for free on George Washington's birthday.

My father and I were big fans of the Washington Senators Baseball Team, which often broke my heart. It was said about the Senators as the team of Washington that "The city was first in war, first in peace, and last in the American League." One year my father also won tickets to the Washington Redskins football games, which I enjoyed right before I went off to Notre Dame.

Among the many worlds of Washington are the numerous embassies of various countries from around the world. Many of these are concentrated on Massachusetts Avenue and surrounding streets. And there are the various higher education institutions like Georgetown, George Washington, Catholic University, American University, Gallaudet College, and UDC. Among great religious pilgrimage sites for visitors are the Shrine of the Immaculate Conception on the Catholic University campus and the National Cathedral on Wisconsin Avenue.

From my youth, I have great memories of dramatic parades, which would bring together various military detachments. Probably the biggest that I ever attended was when General Douglas MacArthur came back from Korea, after the Korean War. A song was written at the time, "Old Soldiers Never Die, They Just Fade Away." I didn't know much about the politics of the War, but in my eyes, at the time, he was a national hero.

Later in my life, I was present for Martin Luther King's "I Have a Dream" speech on the steps of the Lincoln Memorial as well as for the riots after King was assassinated. I have seen or participated in various protest marches, including the March on the Pentagon.

When I was younger, I never would have imagined that someday I would have the pleasure of eating breakfast, lunch, and dinner at the White House or visiting Camp David, or being present in the Rotunda of the Capitol as one of the speakers when Fr. Ted Hesburgh received the Congressional Gold Medal.

I think I have seen the best and the worst in what the city has to offer. From the cherry blossoms to Georgetown nightlife in the summer, to the vibrancy of renovated sections of the city, to the construction of the Metro subway system, to the renovated Union Station, to memorials honoring the fallen military of the Vietnam and Korean Wars, Martin Luther King, Jr., President Franklin Delano Roosevelt, and the WWII veterans. The city is always changing and always a great pleasure to return to.

I would summarize my relationship with my hometown as one of great affection, and every time I have the opportunity to return, I experience a real inner thrill.

Predictions

As I look to the future, based on having lived into my seventies and experienced a lot of life, I am willing to defend the following propositions about the future:

❀ *The role of women in American society will continue to evolve*—The United States is unusual among the developed countries in that we have not yet had an American president who is a woman. However, the percentage of women in the Congress continues to rise and we have had women governors and leaders in the various state legislatures as well as mayors and other participants in the political process. We have also had many distinguished women presidents in higher education. There are also a growing number of women CEO's of major corporations and women's breakthroughs in the sciences are noteworthy. The challenge for women going forward will continue to be how to find balance among the different obligations that go with professional life, private life, and family life. I am confident that the women I have taught at Notre Dame are well prepared to reflect about different styles of life in the future and ways in which they can model a new notion of what it means to be a full female participant in the common life.

❀ *The two greatest American internal problems will remain the race issue and the great economic divide between the richest and the poorest*—We have seen in my lifetime noteworthy progress when it comes to the realities of black life in the post-Civil Rights era. We have had a black president and black leaders in a whole host of areas. However, American demographics continue to change over time. Even if there were no new members of our society through immigration, we would still see a dramatic shift in the composition according to the traditional racial categories. While this is distributed differently according to geography, the basic reality is that the new America will be multi-racial, whether everyone likes it or not. If you add on the correlation between race and economic prosperity, we continue to need to struggle with the percentage of our population that can look forward to the future with hope and a sense of possibility. The gap between the haves and the have-nots has grown exponentially.

❊ *The institution of the family will continue to be challenged*—There are many hopeful signs, including the new stress on intimacy and respect for the individual. It is no longer acceptable for violence to take place between a husband and wife or for children to be undernourished or forced to live in a dysfunctional context. There are many efforts to strengthen the nature of family life—through education, support groups, religiously affiliated preparation programs, and the existence of social networks designed to support the quality of family life. On the other hand, we have a high divorce rate, many young people enter into temporary relationships without marrying, some families feel isolated from their peers, and there is a persistent conflict across generations.

❊ *The American political process will require new models of integrity and responsibility*—There is an increased participation in the political process by women, members of minority groups, young people, and those who really want to make a difference in the quality of the common life. Even the recognition of the existence of corruption in some areas of government is the first step in the process of reform. Efforts to get out and vote, to encourage people to run for office, and to celebrate the quality leadership of some who have been elected to office in the past are all steps in the right direction. But all of that comes up against a sometimes-pervasive public indifference, a distrust of the motivation of some of the reformers, and a kind of fleeing into a smaller community context instead of a concern for the larger common good.

❊ *Higher Education will cease being the automatic step after high school*—More and more we are recognizing that with a great set of educational opportunities available in our country, not everyone needs to go to college in whatever form that might be possible. Some are better off going through specialized training programs or volunteering for the military or otherwise seeking alternate career paths. One of the disincentives is the increased cost for education and the lack of jobs when we have a surplus of degrees in certain areas of study.

❀ *The Christian churches will discover that their common heritage is more important than their historical conflicts*—There is a deep and increased spirit of cooperation among the Christian churches. This takes place not only at the local church level, but also in theological education and in common pursuit of issues that are considered critical for the good of society and the good of the Church. On the negative side, we sometimes have continued pettiness or poor ministerial leadership or an occasional reopening of old wounds.

❀ *The Christian Gospel of Love, Peace, Justice, Forgiveness and Unity will continue to offer the world an alternative to hatred, violence, injustice, revenge, and divisiveness*—Many Christian disciples, in the spirit of the Gospel, are working on concrete problems in a collaborative spirit. In a world that has too much violence, discord, and negativity, the Christian Gospel is full of the spirit of hope and resurrection faith. We do not have to be utopians to believe that we can make a difference in this world and that, with proper commitment and leadership, we can be agents of transformation in the spirit of the Gospel.